The Breakout

by Kate Pollard

the big Blake project

Published by The Big Blake Project

49 Aldwick Road,

Bognor Regis

West Sussex

PO22 7BX

www.thebigblakeproject.org.uk

Printed and bound in Great Britain by Impressions, Cambridgeshire

ISBN **978-0-9933385-0-4**

Dedicated to the Pioneers

who walked off the map

for us

Recommendations:

I read this back to back with the first book - The Brightness. I'm so glad this sequel was available by then as I honestly could not put either book down. This is a tale of supernatural fantasy in the genre of C S Lewis and Tolkien in the best possible way. Not copying, simply undeniable story-telling talent. Characters are created of young people within a plot that not only do you like, but believe in, and want to be part of their adventure. But don't be misled into thinking the appeal is for any one generation. Breakout and its prequel has an ageless and timeless appeal that rightfully should find its way onto the big screen. I will be eagerly looking out for any future offering from this talented author, and hope that much more is heard from this hugely imaginative mind. (Lynette Leitch, Canaan Press)

A riveting read. Kate has captured the creative capacity of the imagination within the realms of the Spirit. She showcases the power of our agreement with whatever we focus on, to deliver either captivity and bondage or fullness and freedom. This book delivers amazing insights and understanding of the current exciting spiritual climate.
Lindy Strong (Freedom Centre, Totnes)

"Today your work begins, to warn the nations and the kingdoms of the world. In accord with my words spoken through your mouth I will tear down some and destroy them, and plant others, nurture them, and make them strong and great."

Jeremiah 1:10 (TLB)

Chapter 1: The Forecast

"More of the same, I'm afraid," apologised Carol, the weather presenter - although it was hardly her fault. Xander roused himself and reached for the remote control to switch off another dismal forecast to round off another depressing day of news. His exams were over, it was mid June and he should be out enjoying his freedom with his mates. This should be the best Summer of his life. Instead, he was sat indoors on a cold, grey, uncharacteristically poor - even for England - June morning. He felt as though the weather had permeated his skin and bone, turning him in to a monochrome version of himself. It was as if a permanent lump of cold metal sat in his abdomen, occasionally pulsing out a frigid, acid wave through his core. How could he rouse himself? What should he do?

His thoughts turned to Scarlett whom he hadn't seen for several weeks now. He had heard from Jess, her personal assistant, that Scarlett's mother had passed away at the end of May and the helplessness and anger he had felt at the news welled up in him afresh. He reached for his phone and looked her up in his contacts as he had done numerous times before. He opened a text page and stared at it for a few moments before closing it again and throwing the phone petulantly into the corner of the sofa where the arm met the seat.

"What's the use?" He spoke out loud, surprised by the sound of his own voice. Then he rose from the sofa and headed for the kitchen to perform his ritual cupboard opening performance.

Chapter 2: Grief

Scarlett looked across the shiny, marble top of the kitchen island in her parents' home at the man she hardly knew; her father. He had shrunk, physically it seemed, since the sudden loss of his wife. They had been doing this standoff dance for a couple of weeks and she was tired of it.

"What can I do, Dad?" she asked, shrugging and holding up her hands helplessly.

He looked up from the cup of tea he had been staring in to. "What?" he asked, vaguely.

"Talk to me!"

"Scarlett? Is that you Dear?" He didn't look at her, just through her, it seemed; in to the distant past where this pain was not even a fleeting thought.

Scarlett had to confess she was surprised by her father's reaction to his wife's death. She had always thought of him as a cold, unfeeling man. A part of her was angry with him for selfishly indulging in such emotions now. Why could he not have shown her mother this love while she was alive? Perhaps he had. She had to admit she didn't really know them, either of them, anymore. The Collective had been such a massive part of her life for the past few years that she had had little time for anything else. A pang of guilt accompanied this thought and regret. She looked at the old man standing in the kitchen, once again staring in to his teacup. She wished he could be the strong, emotionally stunted man she had always believed him to be right now; it would certainly make this easier.

"What's the use?" she uttered, childishly, turning on her heel and walking out of the room; away from the claustrophobic hopelessness of grief and shattered dreams and out in to the cold, grey June day and a world she didn't recognise anymore.

Chapter 3: The Ultimate Phase

Peter Nixon sat in his office in the House of Commons. He stretched out his legs under the desk and crossed his ankles, leaning back in the ludicrously expensive chair he had purchased to reward himself for the way things had progressed. He brought his fingers together in a steeple, spreading them wide and pressing both of his index fingers in to his lips, which had curled in to a self-appreciative smile.

Nixon had no one and wanted no one to depend upon for affirmation. He was unwavering in his self-sufficiency - had been since his childhood in an orphanage. He had never looked in to the reason for which he had been placed in such an institution; that was the past and it held no interest for him. The future, that was his goal, and it had been since he was a young boy making a grown up and desperately sad decision not to wait for the perfect couple to come along and welcome him - in a golden glow of 1950s Hollywood schmaltz - in to their perfect lives and their perfect home, to become the perfect family. He made the choice to close his heart to love and a family embrace, deciding instead to rely on himself and resist all attempts to graft him in to someone else's misguided views about what constituted a happy childhood. This way was better; this way he knew who to trust. This way, no one but Peter Michael Nixon could take credit for his success.

And what a success he was! Prime Minister of Great Britain; national saviour of the people; leader of the Collective - a movement of young people intent on affecting their lives and society for the greater good (or so they thought!) He looked out of the window at the dismal sky. The contrast that was evident between that aspect and the view from the windows in the Castle when the Brightness had been at its height less than a year ago was stark, but it did not even occur to him. Peter Nixon had never been impressed by the Brightness; had never been touched by the pure and intoxicating pull of that benevolent force as they had all partnered with it to such glorious and remarkable effect. He didn't see it because it did not interest him. He served a different master, followed a completely opposite vision and did not possess the least desire to see Scarlett's goals achieved.

Scarlett Tang. He smirked to himself as a fighter might at the memory of seeing his adversary on the mat. He hadn't thought about her for a few days. Since phasing her out of the Castle - that was how he saw it, as she had served her purpose - he did not need to waste time considering her. He owed her nothing! It wasn't personal, she was naive and he had exploited that as any predator would. He felt no qualms, his vision was merely bigger than hers.

About a month ago, he had leaked her mother's illness to the press. Simultaneously, he had called a meeting of the Collective and Shapeshifter - his loyal guide and companion - had given an Oscar-winning performance to the children, explaining her need at this time to step down from leadership. This was the meeting that Xander had inadvertently stumbled upon on his return to the Castle. Nixon congratulated himself as he thought about how easily this phase of his plan had been fulfilled. After Scarlett's departure, his guides had diluted the memories of her involvement in the minds of the children they partnered with.

And so, Scarlett Tang, creator of the greatest social movement in modern history, became little more than a footnote in the minds of those who still attended the Collective. It was Nixon's intention that her past success would also be condemned to oblivion as he established a new order and robbed, not just the past, but the future hope as well from the nation he served.

Chapter 4: Rosie

Ping.

Xander reached languorously for his phone and swiped the screen. He was in his default position - lying on his bed, left knee bent, right arm hanging over the edge, staring at the ceiling. It was a message from Rosie.

'Hey Xander. How's it going? Wanna hang out? Rosie.'

He tried to make himself think coherently, to come up with some reason or excuse for avoiding her. Suddenly, he realised with a start, he felt the need for company; personal contact. He was tired of going round and round in his own head trying to come up with a solution to what had happened to the Collective. He felt responsible somehow, like he had a calling on him to make it right. It was a ridiculous notion and he had tried to shake it, but he couldn't.

'Yours or mine?' He found himself typing in response. His finger hovered for a moment over 'send' before he pressed it. He felt a surge of relief that he was finally making contact with someone else, and he was glad it was Rosie. She was a good friend, non-judgemental and kind.

There was a pause, in which he stirred and sat up, rubbing his hands vigorously over his face to dispel the torpor and trying to get his head together.

'Mine.'

He was a little surprised and felt his eyebrows involuntarily shoot up. In the eighteen months he had known Rosie in this capacity as fellow mind-travellers, she had never once suggested they meet there. A few times she had come round to his home, but usually they had met at school or in Scarlett's office.

'Ok. Where is mine?' he asked, electronically.

She texted him her address and ten minutes later Xander was walking the short distance to her house. He turned up the collar on his jacket to keep out the chill wind that blew - that seemed to have blown for months. Meteorologists were stumped by it and used words like 'unprecedented'. They couldn't put this one down to the Jet Stream! But Xander knew where it came from. This particular ill wind had been blowing since their last attempt to access the Castle had been foiled and their separation from the Brightness had become permanent. He looked up at the dark clouds which seemed to hang over the nation like a putrid fog. They reminded him of the clouds that had obliterated the light and warmth in the place he had visited nearly every day; the place he loved; the place where dreams had become possible. He felt sadness for the loss of it. For the thousandth time he wondered if there was another way to access the Brightness and restore order, to defeat Peter Nixon and the demonic powers he had harnessed to do his bidding. For the thousandth time, as he turned in to Rosie's driveway, he felt overwhelmed by the fact that he had absolutely no idea.

Chapter 5: Disorganised Chaos

Rosie answered the door before the echo of the chimes had faded. She looked different out of uniform and it reminded him how much of their friendship had been based around school. Indeed, how much of his life had been focused on the Collective to the point where he hadn't socialised or pursued a life away from it for so long. He wasn't angry about it, how could he be? It had given him so much. He was grateful for it and for Rosie's friendship. But it made him wonder if he needed to find more of a balance in his life, get to know Rosie without the framework of the Collective to base everything on. He wondered to himself, as he looked at her, if life would now return to something like normal, whatever that was, and he realised that being a teenager and doing teenage things with friends like Rosie and Dan wouldn't be such a bad thing after all. If this ride he, no they, had been on had suddenly come to an end; well, he would survive it. Secretly though, seeing Rosie again standing on her doorstep, fresh-faced and dressed in casual clothes, stirred something up in him. In spite of his best attempts to convince himself that this was enough, Xander knew more than ever that he would not rest until he had done everything in his power to try to restore what had been lost.

She looked a little coy, he thought, standing there for the couple of moments it had taken for the sensory overload he had just experienced to cross his consciousness. He smiled at her to put her at her ease.

"Come in," she invited, stepping to one side. "Excuse the mess."

In an instant he realised why she had not invited him before. Her house was in stark contrast to his own. At home, with just the three of them, everything had its place and clutter was kept to a minimum. The odd book lying around or a stray pair of shoes. This was chaos. The hallway alone was home to a double buggy, an infinite number of shoes - none of which, at first glance, appeared to have a partner - pegs with coats of various sizes, boxes of nappies, brightly coloured plastic toys in varying states of repair and a selection of overflowing baskets which appeared to be someone's misguided and quite obviously failed attempt at some point or other, to bring order in to the craziness. It was quiet though, he was grateful for that. This was so alien to him and he realised he was probably a bit of a neat freak.

"Where is everyone?" he asked, trying to distract himself from the mess.

If Rosie had seen the expression of discomfort on his face, then she hid it well, answering him breezily, "Dad's at work, my sisters are at school - I still haven't quite got used to the fact that it's ok to be here on a school day! - and Mum has taken the twins to toddler group." Rosie's parents had discovered they were expecting twins having thought their existing family of three girls was complete. It had not been plain sailing as Ryan had been very poorly at birth. But, thanks to their visualisations in the early days of the Castle, he had made a full recovery. Now both of them were full of energy and mischief and Rosie often had Xander laughing at tales of their antics.

They went through in to the kitchen/diner which seemed even more disorganised. There were still breakfast pots and cereals on the table, along with a four pint carton of blue-topped milk with the lid off. More dishes lay in the sink and on the draining board. He was surprised Rosie didn't struggle with the mess, she struck him as very neat and ordered in herself. Maybe she ignored it to maintain her sanity. If this was the case, then he felt honoured that she had asked him here as it revealed a deep level of trust. He felt a little ashamed that he had instantly and inconsiderately made a judgement about her home, and decided in that moment not to let it matter.

"Do you want a drink or anything?"

He glanced involuntarily at the glasses on the draining board that were being given the car wash brush treatment by a tortoiseshell cat and realised that his acceptance of Rosie's living arrangements was still a work in progress!

"No, I'm ok thanks," he replied, smiling graciously to conceal his anxiety.

They went through to the living room. Cbeebies was muted on the television. Rosie hunted for the remote for a while, before turning it off at the plug. She brushed some toys, biscuit crumbs and discarded popper vests off the sofa and motioned for him to sit. He obliged, perching on the seat.

"How've you been?" she asked, looking at him with a mixture of concern and compassion. He obviously hadn't concealed the weight of responsibility from her.

"So, so," he replied, playing it down; the corners of his mouth turning down as he tipped his head from side to side.

"Have you heard from anyone?"

He knew by 'anyone', she meant had he heard from Scarlett. "No," he replied.

They sat in silence for a while, each lost in their own thoughts. Then Rosie reached for a half-drunk glass of orange squash and held it tightly in her hand. She stared absentmindedly at it without raising it to her lips. "Is it over, do you think?" she asked him, presently, looking up. Her voice sounded small and distant, yet something in it was imploring him to contradict her.

"I don't know," he replied, truthfully, looking her straight in the eyes. "I hope not."

"Should we try to contact her? Scarlett, I mean," Rosie asked, holding his gaze.

"Not yet. What would be the point? She's got enough to deal with, you know, with her mum and everything."

"Yes, of course," she broke eye contact momentarily, looking down at the floor, "you're right. We can't do nothing though, can we?" Again that look he had seen before, challenging him, 'You're the leader here Xander, what are you going to do? Please don't let us down!' That was what her eyes said, even if her mouth had let him off the hook. As much as it annoyed him and made him want to have a teenage tantrum and chuck his toys out of the pram, Xander knew it was the truth. The Brightness had chosen him, that was the conclusion he was rapidly coming to. It had chosen him and it was not enough to sit here, paralysed by doubts and self pity.

"What are you going to do about it Xander?" The question was as clearly posed in his head as if someone had spoken out the words to him.

"I'm going to find the Brightness, somehow Rosie. It's out there still, I know it is. You're right. It isn't over, not till I say it is!"

Xander stood up and as he did so, he felt a surge of something he hadn't experienced for a while. Hope.

Chapter 6: Come Clean

Xander's father had come home early. The restaurant was dead and there was little point in staying open. People didn't seem to be eating out these days. A general malaise had descended upon the country and people had entrenched back in to their own bunkers, separating themselves from each other and preserving what little independence they had left after all of the recent anti-terror legislation. His dad, Ric, looked older and more drawn than Xander had ever seen him - like his own father, Nico, who had died relatively young from cancer. This thought immediately worried Xander as he did not want to see history repeat itself; particularly as there was no way to access the Brightness at the moment to intercede against such a dreadful thing, as they had successfully done with Mrs Berkley his Year 10 tutor. It made him feel all the more keenly the loss of such a privilege. It is when you are most in need that you want to have the reassurance of a higher power to turn to and Xander could not entertain at this moment even the possibility that his father might get sick and he wouldn't be able to help.

They were all sitting in the living room with the television monotonously murmuring away in the background. The news was on, but nobody really wanted to give it their full attention as it comprised of nothing but horror stories about assaults, foreclosures, redundancies and recession.

"This country's going to the dogs!" his father growled, bad temperedly.

"Turn it off then, Love," urged Lana, his wife.

"What's happened to this place?"

"Think where we would be if Peter Nixon hadn't stepped in to take the reins?"

Xander responded without thinking, still feeling vulnerable from the shock of seeing his father look so ill, "That bastard? Are you serious?"

"Xander!" His mum looked shocked. In fact, she couldn't have looked more shocked if he had slapped her across the face. He was not in the habit of speaking like that in front of his parents and he instantly regretted his outburst.

"Sorry," he mumbled.

"Where did that come from?" asked his dad. He was looking at him searchingly. Xander was usually so mild mannered and unflappable.

Xander sat there, staring at his hands, which seemed to be squirming in his lap like creatures independent of his body. He felt a little ashamed, plus he hated keeping things from his parents as they usually had such a close bond and that was one of the things he loved about them. But he knew this was not the time for confessions such as: "Mum, Dad, I've got something to tell you. All the time you thought I was at study groups and after school clubs, I was operating high up in an organisation called the Collective which harnessed the positive thoughts of children for the benefit of personal and community transformation!" No, he couldn't do it. It was there on the tip of his tongue, desperate to unburden him, but an invisible barrier held the words back, strangling them in his throat. He took a deep breath and settled for the more palatable, yet still believable, muttered response of, "I just hate politicians, they're all the same. A bunch of self-serving power freaks."

"I think that's a bit harsh, Love. Nixon has done a lot to get this country back on its feet after the terror attack."

A few months ago, Nixon succeeded in removing certain key members of Parliament by using one of his spirit guides to access the Commons and plant a strategic bomb. It was so specific as to allow him to replace the Prime Minister unchallenged, and put various sympathisers to his cause into important cabinet positions. Of course, the nation was oblivious to his malevolent plans and any attempt to expose him would be in vain as he had covered his tracks so well and made himself indispensible to the people. Ironically, he was now viewed by the public as the hero of the hour and there was nothing they would not follow him through. Xander particularly hated the fact that his mum had been so deceived by this monstrous man. He desperately wanted to tell her the truth about him, but he knew it would come out sounding like paranoid nonsense.

"I'm going to bed," he resigned, getting up abruptly before he said something else he might regret. He left the lounge without saying goodnight and headed upstairs to his room.

Chapter 7: Olam

Xander lay awake long after his parents had gone to bed. He felt bad about his outburst, but seeing the extent of their deception made him all the more determined to find a way to make things right.

He wished he could go to the Castle and engage with the vivid, playful light they had come to call the Brightness. He had never really thought about it before, but he found himself musing, suddenly, about the origin of the name; whether it was something Scarlett had come up with to describe the light which resided in her creation or if, maybe, the light had come first, already bearing the name, and drawn her there to experience it. He made a mental note to try to remember to ask her when things became more settled. He smiled as he recalled the happy times there. The Brightness always seemed so benevolent; so keen to guide them to want the best and to help them see it for themselves.

"I don't know if you can hear me, Brightness," he found himself saying, out loud, "but I'm talking to you. How can I find you? I don't believe this is over but I need you to show me the way. I want to fight for the truth." It seemed funny, talking to himself, and it made him feel self-conscious, but he didn't know what else to do. He waited, straining his senses to examine the darkness which surrounded him. His eyes, his ears, the hairs on his skin even, all made a supreme effort to intercept the tiniest alteration in his environment. Nothing seemed to respond to his request. A peace filled his heart though, reassuring him that he had made a start, set his foot on the path - whatever that was.

Eventually Xander drifted off to sleep, where he dreamed of an ancient pathway with a crossroads in it. A man stood at the junction beneath a sign with four arms. He looked at the man and asked him which way he should take. The man did not speak, but Xander could sense something about him which made him feel instantly connected. He felt like he had met him before in some other worldly place and was drawn by the deep wisdom in his eyes. The man lifted his right hand and pointed up at the signpost, to the arm which read 'Olam'. Nodding his thanks, Xander struck out on the path leading off to the left.

The terrain seemed unnaturally difficult to walk upon and Xander found he had to look down at the ground because his feet were forever stumbling on awkward rocks embedded in the narrow track. His surroundings seemed heath-like and remote when he glanced up to check what lay ahead. Strangely, in the way that only a dream can behave, the path seemed to respond to his vexation by becoming increasingly steep and treacherous. Progress had become so slow that he was beginning to wonder if he would actually get anywhere at all.

"Look up."

It was a voice, clear as anything, and his body seemed to absorb the sound, sending ripples of vibration through every cell. It startled him as there seemed to be nobody about. Xander paused in his dream and looked up again, forcing his gaze off the tricky path.

"Now try," urged the voice.

Try what? Walking? Xander put one foot in front of the other and discovered that, as he looked up, each footstep became progressively easier until he almost felt as though he was flying along the path with his feet barely touching it. It felt familiar, like other flying dreams he had experienced in the past - although he had dismissed them back then as childish fantasy. There was a lesson here somewhere, he thought to himself, and laughed with the exhilaration of the moment. He glanced down to see what the path looked like now, but immediately stumbled and fell awkwardly on to a jagged rock.

"Ow!" he exclaimed, examining his knee, upon which a lump with an angry looking graze was swelling almost before his eyes.

"Look up," reiterated the voice, firmly and patiently.

Gingerly at first, but with gathering confidence, Xander progressed with increasing speed along the path. Presently he noticed that a stream had started to run parallel to his track. As he looked at it, to his surprise he was no longer travelling along the path, but had effortlessly crossed over to the stream and was now progressing up it with the same swiftness and dexterity. He laughed as he skimmed across the surface of the water. It had the same sparkling qualities as the Brightness, he noticed, and he reached down with his left hand to scoop up some water as he ran. It glowed in his cupped hand, alive with rainbow luminescence and instinctively he drew it to his lips and drank. The cool sensation of the water was invigorating and empowering, and he laughed again, scooping up more and more water and drinking it thirstily.

He felt joyful and playful and dove down in to the water to immerse himself completely. It was incredible; he could breathe and see with such clarity through the crystal waters. It felt viscous, like oil and he slipped through it without resistance, moving with the grace and alacrity of a dolphin. As he broke the surface again, Xander noticed a waterfall in front of him and he stopped, bobbing in the pool of water below it, wondering what to do next.

Xander looked around him and noticed a sign beside the waterfall. In true dream fashion, it did not seem the least bit unusual to see it there. The sign read 'Tikkun Olam', but it meant nothing to Xander, although he knew instinctively that it was important.

He also knew that he could not go any further at this time. His visit here was to inspire him, to show him a different level of operating in the Brightness and it was time to turn back - although it was with no small amount of disappointment that he retraced his steps. He lay on his back, supported by the water as if a thousand tiny hands held him gently and securely. The sky above him was cloudless and blue. He instantly thought of the Castle and felt a pang of sadness mixed in with the familiarity of these sensations. He knew that this place was somehow connected with the realm he had travelled to with such fondness and frequency over so many months. It felt the same somehow. The Brightness, albeit in a different form, was here, he just knew it.

Suddenly Xander bumped to a halt. The stream just stopped at the bank. He pulled himself out, marvelling at the fact that he did not appear to be wet and looked around, wondering where he was. It felt familiar. He looked down and recognised the path he had initially been on. A jagged looking rock glistened in the bright light and he bent down to study it more closely. Blood. His blood. It was the rock he had stumbled on, he knew it.

At that moment, Xander awoke with a start. The dream had left such a strong impression on all of his senses that, for a moment, it felt completely real and he half imagined himself still there. He continued to feel the water, the warmth, the path beneath his feet;

could still smell the heather and the clean, clear atmosphere. The word 'Olam' drifted in his mind's eye and he quickly roused himself and turned on the bedside light, before scrabbling for his notepad and pen to write it down. He mentally relived the dream from start to finish, surprised by the clarity of his recall. The one thing which eluded him however, was the name of the waterfall he had seen and it frustrated him. And why had the stream stopped at that point? With a sudden moment of clarity he saw the rock on the path. Wondering and doubting his next decision, Xander found himself peeling back the covers and examining his legs. His left knee carried an ugly welt with broken skin which had bled on his covers. His jaw dropped in incredulous wonder.

Chapter 8: Research

Xander glanced at the glowing red digits of his alarm clock - 3:33. He was still buzzing from the dream and felt wide awake. He got up and grabbed his laptop, powering it up as he arranged the pillows behind his back as a makeshift chair. He waited impatiently for the desktop to load, then clicked on the search engine as soon as the machine had finished booting up.

'Olam', he keyed in, unsure of what would appear. It came up with a list of businesses and he was momentarily disappointed. He refined his investigation to look for the meaning of the word and a further search revealed something which shocked him. Olam meant an ancient way, everlasting and eternal, yet hidden. But there was more:

"Tikkun Olam - repairing, healing, perfecting the world," he read out loud, instantly recognising the name of the waterfall in his dream. What did this mean? He was baffled, exhilarated and a little frightened all in one go. He lay back against the pillows and thought it through, his heart thudding in his chest. He remembered what he had asked before he had gone to sleep. Could it be that the Brightness was speaking to him? Showing him something as he slept? Was it literal or symbolic? He thought for a while, sensing his brain feverishly searching for something to compare it to; he drew a blank.

"Let's think about this," he said in a hushed tone, no longer feeling awkward about speaking out loud, but finding it strangely soothing and reassuring. "It could represent my journey, that makes sense. The path could be where I learned to operate with the Brightness and the point I stumbled is where it all went wrong." He paused for a while, sensing on some level that he was on the right lines. "That would suggest that the stream is about a new way of encountering the Brightness and the waterfall is about what is to come - the healing of the nations!" He felt excited now and adrenaline coursed through his system.

"Wow! That's huge! Could it be that?" If he was right, then what lay ahead of him was far larger than anything he could have imagined. He felt so small and insignificant, sitting there in his bed in the early hours of the morning, trying to process something which appeared to be of truly epic proportions.

"Why did I come back down it?" He scratched his head, puzzled, but keen to think about something which felt more manageable.

"Because this is where you are now. You haven't got there yet."

Did he think that on his own? Did he even say it? He heard it, deep down in himself, the way he had sometimes heard the Brightness talking to him. He looked at his knee again. "This is where I am now," he repeated, accepting his position and letting the words find their level in his comprehension. It felt good to know where he stood, but with that came the knowledge that there was so much more to come, and that was an entirely different matter.

Chapter 9: A Brief Encouragement

Xander managed to sleep again after his night of excitement. When he awoke, it was late morning and something felt different. It took him a while to recognise exactly what it was because he was sluggishly trying to force his brain to process the events of that night. He half expected to wake up disbelieving it somehow, or feeling a strong sense of anti-climax - things often feel more heightened and dramatic under the cover of darkness, he had experienced this before with dreams, pulling on your emotions and magnifying your senses in a way that the daylight hours often fail to achieve as thoroughly. Surprisingly though - and this was where the experience differed from a regular dream - it was as fresh and vivid as he remembered it during the night. More real than reality, if that was at all possible, and that was exhilarating and a little alarming.

As his physical senses caught up with his brain, Xander remembered his knee and examined it afresh in the cold light of day. That was the moment that he realised what it was that was different about today, compared with every other morning he had woken up for what seemed like months; the sun was shining through his curtains!

Forgetting his knee, which had started to scab over, Xander jumped up, strode across his room and, stretching his arms wide in a gesture of supplication, threw open both curtains together with such force that he almost brought down the rail. He closed his eyes, tipped back his head, inhaled deeply though his nose, then sighed out through his mouth.

"Hello sun!" he exclaimed, laughing at his own stupidity, but unable to contain the joy he felt from feeling the warmth of this particular celestial body on his own. He heard the sound of children out on the street and in their gardens, laughing and shouting playfully. It was as if everyone had simultaneously been released from their enforced incarceration and he realised that the sound had been absent for too long. Forgetting about the heaviness of the last few weeks and months; the oppressive darkness and the desperation of a nation that had almost started to feel like his own personal burden, Xander ran downstairs and out in to the garden in his pyjama shorts. It is remarkable how a little sunshine acts as a drug on your system, a legal high; a natural intoxication. He looked up in to the sky and the blueness above him reminded him of the Castle. What he had not been able to see from his window, however, was that it was only a result of a break in the clouds. It was as if a tear had been made in the dense cauldron of cloud that had settled over the nation and he was at its centre. Like the parting of the red sea, huge banks of cloud appeared to be held back to enable him to see beyond, in to a perfect sky.

He lay on his back on the grass and looked up. He could not shake the ludicrous suggestion rattling around his consciousness that this was for him. It was a glimmer of hope, a spotlight on the deep and limitless potential which lay in the future and as soon as he saw it, grasped it and processed it as truth, the cloud rolled back in, decreasing the aperture with the speed and efficiency of a giant drawing his purse strings together, to shut out the sun.

Xander sighed and stayed there for a while, thinking about what he had just witnessed. It was a sign, he knew it, there was hope and he must persevere. But with the fading sunlight and gathering gloom he again fell under the spell of lethargy and dismay; disappointment and lost hope.

"Where ever do I start?" he asked the universe, as it mocked him silently. A sixteen year old boy with a dream but no vision, a hope but no plan.

"You're going to have to do better than that!" he challenged.

Chapter 10: The Collective

Scarlett Tang had been ahead of her time, she was a visionary with a social conscience. Many people look at what is wrong in the world and offer comments or judgements on how it can be solved or what should be done, but only a very few actually rise up and attempt to do something about it. Scarlett was one of the few. In fact, even among the few, Scarlett was unique. She had gone way beyond offering an opinion or an alternative, or even affecting a community or changing the lives of a marginal group of people within a community. As altruistic as that was, that kind of change generally sprung from an experience of intense loss or personal tragedy. She was unusual because she wanted to implement something which would tackle society head on; challenge its weaknesses; inspire it with hope; offer it a solution and all through the motivation of young people. She was more than a catalyst, she was inspirational. People believed in Scarlett Tang and had followed her in to the conception and launch of her instrument of salvation - the Collective.

In many ways it was a simple concept which involved a few key ingredients: hope, unity, vision and the Brightness. She had gradually engaged children - largely of secondary school age - to partner with her in a mystical Castle where they would align their minds in collective visualisation to hope for, and call for, an end to social injustice, community impoverishness and family fractures. It had worked; it was beautiful in its simplicity as the children could gather together in rooms designated for specific transformations and call on the benevolent involvement of the Brightness - a light source that revealed itself in the windows of the rooms like stained glass, displaying the full colour spectrum with an energy that was alive with possibility. The Brightness was able to respond to their requests and simultaneously drive them; forming a bridge between the supernatural realm in which the Castle existed and the natural world they inhabited, whereupon their hopes took on a physical shape and became reality. Transformation followed and people were happy and secure, until Peter Nixon systematically stole those simple ingredients, highlighted before, and replaced hope with fear; unity with mistrust; vision with despair and the Brightness itself with a dark and insidious force, fed by the worship of Moloch - an ancient demonic god - and assisted by a carefully selected group of dark servants, willing to go to any lengths to see the Brightness shut down.

When he first assumed the mantle of leadership, Nixon relied heavily on the deception of one of his spirit guides - Shapeshifter - who took on the physical appearance of Scarlett to ease the transition. She was loved and respected by the children and he would probably have struggled to take over without her apparent blessing. Her mother's demise was a convenient reason - and a well executed part of Nixon's plan, if the truth be told - for Scarlett to bow out of leadership and pass the reins on to her number two. Few people within the organisation knew of the sinister goings on or the deception they were now under. It was done with such a ring of authenticity that they had no need to question it. However, with the Brightness no longer featuring or regulating the events which took place in the Castle, an altogether more sinister regime was in force. Not only had Nixon succeeded in driving out this benevolent partner, he had introduced a system which did not require collective thinking at all. It was now a complete farce, where members drew their power from a deep well of darkness going back to Moloch himself, but disguised as light-bearing, angelic-looking spirit guides, who were just as adept at engendering negative, paranoid outcomes to visions as the Brightness had been at encouraging the opposite. So subtle was the transition, that people still believed themselves to be operating under the same force as they always had, albeit under slightly different circumstances.

Over the past few weeks since Scarlett's exit and the failure of Xander and the others to regain the upper hand, Nixon had moved swiftly to consolidate his advantage. His prior role as Minister for Education meant that people were whole-heartedly behind his educational policies as Prime Minister. They looked to him with unflinching faith, believing he was their saviour rather than seeing the truth - Peter Nixon had systematically destroyed the social fabric of the nation, undermining all they had seemed to believe in and sold it all back to them as the solution.

Moloch was a god who relished sacrifice - particularly that of children - and so the nation's policy maker made it his priority to start the new academic year with a physical representation of the Collective in every secondary school in the country. He didn't have long to make it happen.

Chapter 11: Foundations

Nixon had been introduced to Moloch by a university professor when he was a young man. Initially - as with many secretive societies - he was unaware of the depths of demonic activity which took place behind the carefully engineered façade. The Order, as it was called, was an ancient organisation that had gone underground in more recent generations, but still retained its potency. In reality, the fact that people believed it to be extinct made it all the more powerful, as members were able to convene and worship Moloch unhindered and unquestioned.

He had not been alarmed by his first encounter with this demonic lord, a gigantic beast of mythical proportions who sat enthroned with arms outstretched to fulfil his continual lust for offerings - particularly that of child sacrifice. His body was that of a man and he had the head of a calf. He was surrounded at all times by a faint sulphurous whiff which many recoiled from if they ever made it in to his presence. Nixon was different, however. He didn't seem to manifest any fear or revulsion where this beast was concerned. He was a single minded man who was in pursuit of a personal quest for power. To what extent his childhood had made him the man he was, was a matter for debate. Although nobody could say for sure, it would have made for an interesting nature versus nurture argument.

Peter Nixon's earliest memories were not something he ever dwelt upon. What was it L.P. Hartley said? 'The past is a foreign country: they do things differently there.' Suffice it to say, they were not happy ones taking him back to days of love and security within a family unit; nor were they traumatic memories of violence or poverty. The truth of the matter was, he didn't go back there in his mind because all he remembered was confusion, abandonment and powerlessness and these were emotions he had long since vowed to eliminate from his life. He had resided in a children's home for as long as he could remember and had keenly felt the isolation and fear as he watched others move on to be fostered or adopted. What it was about that small, lonely, blond haired little boy that caused people to overlook him, nobody at the home could quite put their finger on. But he had a slightly dangerous streak to his personality and a lack of empathy for others which seemed to grow with him to the point where, even the carers at the home were wary of him. He seemed to have decided from a young age to close himself off emotionally and rely on no one but himself, even avoiding any and all forms of personal relationship or connection. He focused all of his attention on his studies with a steely determination for his circumstances not to hold him back in any way.

He left Cambridge University with a first class degree in Politics and a growing presence within the Order. He had learnt how to progress; who to use, who to ignore. He studied people with the same gritty determination that he had used to pursue his education and he could read them with an almost occultic accuracy. He found their vulnerabilities and preyed on them to his own advantage. Where he could not progress under the power of his own charms - for Nixon had developed a strongly convincing façade as a likeable, trustworthy, charismatic leader; he was a veritable chameleon, subtly adapting depending on who he was with - he would engage the assistance of a growing following of demonic guides. Initially, the guides came to him as a gift from Moloch for his service and dedication, but the man had succeeded in manipulating them to serve him over and above the demon king. Such was his power and such was the extent of his unflinching pursuit of his goal. Peter Nixon would not be content until all that was owed to him; all that had scorned and rejected him; all that he sought and desired was under his feet and he ruled over it. Few people in history have sought that kind of power with the fervency that he did and none of them had ever found a way to harness it completely. But Nixon had a plan, he was in this for the long game and he was determined that, by captivating the youth of this generation, he would succeed in establishing a foundation of loyalty and service that would secure his position in the nation for as long as he desired it. Every ruler knows the value of educating the next generation in order to perpetuate their kingdom, but it was the very crux of his vision not just an aspect of it. And who knew where that could ultimately take him?

Chapter 12: The Castle

In its heyday, the Castle had been a place where the children would gather in rooms designed to target elements within society such as family, community, finances and health. About two hundred had found themselves able to not just visualise themselves up in to the Castle by focusing their minds, but to engage with the Brightness for the purposes of positive transformation. Those days were gone. Numbers had remained stable - thanks to Shapeshifter's convincing performance as Scarlett, assuring the children that it was business as usual - but that was where the similarities ended. The Castle was now a relic to the old ways, no longer the warm and inviting haven it had once been. It was now a lump of dull rock, hunched under a brooding sky, the complete antithesis of its original conception. The rooms, once so vibrant with colour and committed to partnership though the notion of the labyrinth, had become a waiting room for the destination that Nixon had since created. From each original room, a corridor led down to a second chamber where the children would individually partner with a guide. There was at least one for each room now as Nixon's army of demons had grown. The Brightness had been replaced by an artificial light source emanating from the guides. Externally, they were beautiful beings, clothed in white and radiance. The children had begun to develop relationships with individual guides, becoming susceptible to their influences. They sought them out, blindly and unknowingly allowing themselves to be manipulated. The success of the transition had even taken Nixon by surprise and he grudgingly had to admit that this was down to Scarlett. She had laid good foundations here by encouraging the children to be masters of their own destiny and follow their own agendas - albeit within benevolent parameters.

Moloch was not an omnipresent god and he frequented the Castle more often than he had visited the building in London which housed the Order. He liked it here. He had long desired to gain access in to this realm. For as long as he had existed, his influence had been limited by certain spiritual layers which formed the structure of the heavenly realms. His realm was just as accessible from the earth as the Castle had been, but there was a distinction which separated him from the realm of the Brightness. He hated the Brightness with an intensity which is rarely demonstrated on the earth. He hated its light; hated its creativity; hated its goodness and had long desired to find a way to penetrate the realm it occupied and snuff it out. He snorted to himself with undisguised delight.

"You have done well, my son." He had an affection for Peter Nixon which he rarely felt for any human. Normally he despised them for their weakness and lack of conviction, but Peter was different and he looked upon him now with the fondness of a parent. Peter picked up on the appellation and understood its significance.

"Do you want me to call you Father?" he joked, looking up at the beast he served. There was a flicker of something in its monstrous eyes. What was it? Pride? Sentiment? Nixon turned away in disgust, disappointed that Moloch had revealed his weakness to him. He thought Moloch understood; thought he knew about lust for power and selfish ambition. It was a turning point in their relationship. It was the moment when servant became master.

Chapter 13: Meanwhile, Back at the Office

The Cabinet Room was stacked in his favour. Peter had been careful to surround himself with people who would be sympathetic to his plans, gradually replacing the more dyed in the wool politicians with those whom he had observed, over the past few months - if not years - to be susceptible to his charm or easily manipulated. Sebastian Eccleston-Wright, a weak-chinned hooray Henry with a public school education and silver spoon firmly lodged where the sun would never shine, had succeeded him as planned as the Minister for Education. He was nice enough, but not the sharpest tool in the shed and Nixon had no problem suggesting what the next pertinent move for national education policy might be. In fact, most of the leading lights in the Cabinet were vulnerable to his hypnotic advances - at least, those whom he viewed to be the most vital to his cause.

It was the beginning of July and they had a little over two weeks to go until Parliament rose for the Summer, not to convene again until early September. Nixon felt the pressure.

"How far have you got with the schools programme, Seb?" he asked with a sickening smile.

"Coming along nicely, Prime Minister," he responded, a little too quickly.

"Are you just telling me what you think I want to hear, or do you have a genuine handle on this?" His gaze was piercing and the Education Minister squirmed, involuntarily.

"Oh no Sir, I assure you," he shook his head fervently then stopped for a moment and nodded, indecisively, not sure in his confusion which response was the correct one.

Nixon turned away and rolled his eyes, gathering his composure. "Idiot," he thought to himself. "And what, exactly, are you assuring me of?" Nixon resisted the temptation to smile at the man's distress.

"We have pushed through a bill which will allow for the Collective to become part of the curriculum. Each school will have a designated room for a guide to occupy full time. I haven't seen any training material for the guides yet though," Seb had gained enough confidence to make this observation.

"Don't worry, that has been taken care of. All of the necessary training has taken place in the Castle so we can relocate to schools." Nixon spoke in such a way that people felt it imprudent to ask too many questions; as though it would be some kind of admission that they weren't smart enough to keep up. It was not that they were afraid of him - that would be disastrous and he would avoid that scenario at all costs - they were in awe of him, simple as that, and his meteoric rise to power. They deferred to his wisdom and experience, not to mention his celebrity status. Around the nation, Nixon was a hero and he was careful to maintain and cultivate this persona, even among the chimps tea party that constituted his Cabinet!

"Very good, Minister. It sounds as if you have it all in hand." Sebastian Eccleston-Wright basked in his master's praise as a dog relishes a ruffle of the ears. "I'm trusting you to ensure that we meet our September deadline."

"You can have my word, Sir," he bowed as he spoke the assurance.

"Good. To other matters then," the Prime Minister suggested.

Chapter 14: The Mystic Secret

Xander had spent the last couple of weeks in relative isolation. He was keen to develop the experiences he had had that night - although it seemed like a lifetime ago - and to research the foundations of the Brightness. It was a slow process, however, as he still didn't know the origin of the name of the supernatural force which manifested itself in the Castle. He knew he needed a revelation similar to that which had occurred in his dream regarding Olam, but it became increasingly apparent to him that the internet was not going to bear fruit here and give him all of the answers he required. The closest he could get to discovering more about a benevolent force using his search engine, was George Lucas's Star Wars. Although it made him smile, it did not inform his search.

His attempts to find out more about Olam were limited but slightly more positive. He discovered it was a Hebrew word which appeared to mean both antiquity and futurity, an everlasting existence. He found it humbling that the place he had visited had been there for all of time and had no qualms about accepting that fact as truth. There also appeared to be a dynamic to it which spoke of concealment and this too made him feel particularly special. What a privilege it was to have been chosen to enter in to a kingdom which was both eternal and hidden from everyday experience. It was exhausting and largely futile work, but it was part of his character to want to gain information and try to understand things both explicitly and implicitly before he could move on to experience based learning. He hated to be unprepared. However, he was beginning to think that the time that was elapsing since his last encounter had taught him a valuable lesson. The Brightness was not something to be understood through study, explicitly or implicitly; it could **only** be experienced. He was worried that he may have wasted valuable time, trying to gather information to either satisfy his own curiosity or lack of knowledge, or allow him to share that knowledge with Scarlett and his friends. It appeared that the Brightness did not want to be understood and imparted, passed on to another as a titbit of interesting statistical data; it wanted to be found. It may have taken Xander a while to come to this conclusion, but it was the key to opening up a whole new realm of possibilities for him. It took him from observer to activist.

Each night, during this dry spell, Xander had gone to sleep hoping to engage with the Brightness or Olam again and each morning he had woken with a sense of anticipation and examined what his memory could recall of his brain's nocturnal activities. It was disappointingly banal or non-existent. But after his epiphany of realisation that he could not study his way into this thing, could not pin it down with any logical thinking, a breakthrough occurred. Xander found himself once again at the cross roads of the Ancient Way. The man he had seen before - at least he assumed he was the same man - stood beneath the arms of the signpost in a stance of endless patience. This time he did not point, he just stood, unflinching and calm.

"Hello," Xander ventured, "who are you? Do you know of the Brightness?"

"I know of it, yes," the man responded. Strangely, his lips did not move but Xander clearly heard him speak.

"What should I do now?" he asked the man.

"Follow your path. Only you can find the Way."

"The way to where? What path? I don't understand." Xander felt confused and a bit desperate. He felt like Alice at the Mad Hatter's Tea Party. He just wanted a straight answer.

"You are designed to see that which is unseeable and to talk to things and cause them to happen. You possess the power of creative words, you must only believe."

"What do you mean?" This wasn't helping, but Xander knew he had been told something of deep significance.

"Follow the path, Xander, it will take you back to the Mystic Secret. There you will learn all you need to know."

"Who are you, did you say?"

"I didn't say. I am Adon Olam, the Overseer. I can guide you, but I am not your destination or your solution. You must find out for yourself. You are Xander, the defender of men, and you were born for such a time as this. Do not believe in what you think you know, but be brave and strike out on the path that has lain hidden for generations. You will unlock the future, Xander, but do not fear the journey. Confucius said, 'A journey of a thousand miles begins with a single step.' Step out."

Suddenly he was wide awake. What a powerful, exhilarating, confusing and overwhelming dream. Xander reached for his journal and wrote down, with as much accuracy as he could, all that had just been shared with him. Any doubts he may have had prior to this moment about the importance of his role in resuming the search for the Brightness had just been soundly dispelled. As much as it terrified him, Xander had to admit that deep down, somewhere in the very marrow of his being, he resonated with this and he knew without a shadow of a doubt that what he had just witnessed was the Truth.

Chapter 15: Scarlett

"How are you doing?" Xander asked, awkwardly. He had finally plucked up the courage to make the call and half expected it to go straight to voicemail.

"So, so. It's not been easy. How about you?" As Scarlett asked the question he heard her voice change from being flat and depressed to warm and concerned.

Xander paused. Where should he start? What actually was going on anyway? Could he explain it? "Can we meet?" he asked, finally.

It was Scarlett's time to pause. She had not seen anyone from the Collective since that fateful day a few weeks back when she had been forced to dismantle the portal which had given them a brief opportunity to revisit the Castle in its intended form - before Nixon had drained the life out of it.

"I don't know . . . . " she hesitated, but Xander could sense she was wavering. "What did you have in mind?"

"Some things have happened recently. I have no framework for them Scarlett. I don't know who else I can talk to about it. When I woke up this morning I just felt I had to call you." There was silence on the other end of the line and Xander felt compelled to fill the gap. "Is that ok?"

"Sorry Xander, of course it is. I just don't know if I'll be of any use to you."

There was another moment of awkwardness in which Xander talked himself in to the fact that Scarlett was about to say no.

"Meet me in my office in an hour," she said with a forcefulness that surprised him. He smiled as he hung up and suddenly noticed that a huge weight seemed to have been lifted from his shoulders.

Chapter 16: Familiar Haunts

It had only been a few weeks since he'd last been to Scarlett's office and he had spent hours there over the past twenty months, but he felt nervous going back. Yet there was a strange familiarity about it, like going back to your old school.

"Hello stranger!" It was Jess, Scarlett's receptionist. She smiled warmly at Xander, standing up and reaching over the desk to give him a little hug.

"Good to see you too," he responded. "Is she in?"

"Arrived about ten minutes ago. Let me buzz her."

Just as Jess picked up the receiver to engage the internal phone, the door to Scarlett's office opened. Xander had to do a double take, just to be sure it was really her. She looked smaller than he remembered and her hair was scraped in to a pony tail. She wore no makeup and was dressed in a simple white t-shirt and skinny jeans.

"Hey you!" she smiled at him. "Come on in." She turned and headed back in to the room and Xander followed her, closing the door behind him.

The room was as he remembered, with the exception that the television, usually on 24/7, was a blank, lifeless screen. She really had cut herself off, he thought.

What had she been going through? He felt awkward again, as though he were invading her privacy and impinging on her grief somehow. Suddenly, his mind was blank and he had nothing to say.

"Would you like a drink or anything?" Scarlett asked, to break the silence, motioning towards the sofa with her hand.

"Oh, no thanks. I'm fine." He sat.

"What's been going on then, in my absence?" she asked, trying to sound breezy.

"I've seen Rosie a couple of times, but no one else. We didn't know what to do."

"I'm sorry, I abandoned you all didn't I?" Scarlett looked mournful and Xander felt her pain.

"No, no," he urged. "I didn't mean that. It's just . . . well, everything changed, didn't it. We all felt a bit lost for a while."

"Has something happened Xander? You said you wanted to talk." Neither of them wanted to get in to a conversation about the way things had ended. No good could come of it from either perspective. It was a tragic loss, but no blame could be attached so it was safer to avoid it altogether and focus on now. Xander was relieved that Scarlett felt it too and had moved their meeting on.

"I do, yes. It has. I'm just thinking where to start. I've thought about this conversation endlessly, but now I'm here . . . . I think I would be better just coming out with it." He took a deep breath and his expression had a definite 'here goes' ring to it. "What do you know about Olam?"

To his relief, she smiled and for the first time in weeks a light went on in her eyes. "You've met him then?" she asked.

Xander exhaled audibly. "I met the Overseer, yes, in a dream. I also dreamed of an ancient way and a waterfall for the healing of the world."

"The baton has been passed." Scarlett sat back, looking proudly at him.

"What do you mean?" This was not what he wanted to hear. Xander had come to her to share the burden, not to have it confirmed to him that this was his race now.

"Don't look so worried. The Brightness has chosen you, Xander. I too had a dream in which Adon Olam told me that he had visited you and would train you up in the ways of the ancients. He called you 'Defender of Men'. I knew he meant you, that's what your name means! Did you know that?"

"I didn't, no." Xander felt humbled. "Will you tell me what you know, Scarlett?"

Chapter 17: A Young Woman's Vision

"Where did you get the original idea from, for the Collective?" Xander asked, curiously. He was bolder now, like they were more than ever on an equal footing and he had a right to be a part of the inception. Months worth of questions and subconscious wonderings found their way to the forefront of his thinking and he was finally able to give them voice.

"I was at university," she looked wistful, as though she had been transported back in her mind to happier times. "You know I've thought about this a thousand times," she looked directly at him, her eyes sparkling with the wonder of an untold revelation, "but I've never succeeded in convincing myself of the absolute, definitive truth. What did come first? Was it my interest in the power of the mind and the huge and untapped resources of the human brain which led me to discover the Brightness? Or was I being directed, all along, down a path which I had been chosen for?" She left the question hanging, but somehow they both knew that Xander's recent experiences, the very existence of another apparently chosen one, made the second option all the more probable.

"I know what you mean," Xander nodded, "I've wondered the same myself. Was I meant to be in that tutorial to hear your first presentation, or did my aptitude for mind travel make me a candidate for this somewhere down the line? I still don't know at what point I became this version of myself, but hearing you speak about the Overseer has made me realise that for some reason, we have a very particular role to play in all of this."

Scarlett let out a brief snort of amusement. "Does it matter in the end **when** we lined up with the programme? We're here now, aren't we! Two individuals walking a similar path, drawn in to something beyond our wildest imaginings."

"So?" Xander inquired, raising a quizzical eyebrow, after an appropriate amount of time had passed. "You were saying?"

"I was fascinated by the research done by Professor Reinholt, a German Professor at my University. His work was focused on impacting physical things with the metaphysical power of positive and negative thinking. It was while I was working with him, excited by the way I saw plant matter flourish under an atmosphere of love and encouragement - for want of a better description - that I started to open my mind to the possibility for social transformation. That, I believe, was when Adon Olam visited me for the first time. I had a dream where I met him in a beautiful place, like nothing I had seen before. It was a land of roads and bridges that intricately wove around and connected in impossible ways. He called it Olam, the land of the everlasting and eternal way and he said I could use it to access a realm of possibility whereby a focal point for collective thought could be established and then accessed from the Earth. He told me to visit often and walk the roads, to get to know the new dimensions and the beings that inhabited them. He called me a pioneer and said I had been chosen to walk off the map of perceived reality. Of course, I didn't know what that meant at the time, but I have certainly experienced it, I can tell you!" She paused and Xander watched a cloud of memory pass across her beautiful face.

"It was a happy time; I was an adventurer. I longed to sleep and travel to the farthest reaches of the Universe. It wasn't just when I slept, either. Sometimes I had a sort of waking vision which was so much like reality I couldn't always tell the difference. I met with wise and creative beings who shared mystical secrets with me. Some of these, I must confess, never made it to my conscious self, but I knew something deep and earth-changing had lodged itself somewhere in the core of my being."

"Did you name the Brightness?"

"No, I was introduced to it originally as Zerah, the Rising Light. But it preferred to be called the Brightness. It just seems right, don't you think?"

Xander nodded. "Why have you never shared any of this before?" He was curious. It would certainly have made his own more recent experiences more measurable; less bizarre.

"It was private; intimate," she smiled and he understood. "We all have to find our own way in to this realm, Xander. I knew that Adon Olam, or the Brightness itself, would find ways to speak to people if it was their wish; just as they spoke to me. I did what I was called to do. I built the Castle. What happened next . . . . Well, I have realised that I can no longer carry the blame for that. Believe me, I've tried. It nearly killed me." She wasn't exaggerating, and in a moment of clarity he could see what it had cost her. She looked up, challenging him with her eyes. "It's your turn now. Don't be afraid of it though, you are more than up to it."

Chapter 18: The Decree

Peter Nixon read through his manifesto one more time to make sure it was completely ready for the September launch. It was a document he was proud of and he smiled to himself with anticipation at the thought of this becoming a reality in a few short weeks.

The Decree, as he liked to call it, was going out to all secondary schools across the country. The concept behind it was that in each school there would be a designated room specifically for children to engage with the Collective. It would be presented as it always had been, a tool for social and personal transformation. He had toyed with the idea of changing the name of the organisation which Scarlett had started, so full of hope - particularly as it no longer fulfilled the brief intimated by the name. There was nothing 'collective' about the current modus operandi. It was now no more than a glorified power channel existing between the misguided and deceived children who partook in the process and the demonic realm, presided over by Moloch. Essentially, a permanent guide would be in residence within the school, physically manifesting as a light bearer. It was entirely possible for a creature which usually inhabited realms other than the earthly one, to become fully visible and physically present within the schools. Their appearance would be replicated over and over as the one children were familiar with seeing in the Castle, through beings such as Naamah. It was felt that this would make the transition that much more simple, as there would be at least one child in most schools by now who had met with these beings in that very place. So whether the children were familiar with the initial concept or not, the Collective could now be established in a more widespread and accessible fashion, reaching much larger numbers than ever before. The ability to be able to mind travel to the Castle was no longer a prerequisite for involvement; but those who had shown the capacity would now become the advocates for the concept within schools, reducing the need for Nixon to have to sell it to them. The aptitude to traverse the spiritual planes in order to operate in the Castle was something Nixon had wanted to eliminate for other reasons apart from accessibility to a much wider audience. What he wanted to control and to squash, was the growing awareness that children had been developing of the realms around them and a natural inquisitiveness to want to explore. Essentially, he was grounding the young who had found their wings and learnt to fly, before they could get a taste for the realms which the Brightness frequented. Without their knowledge, he was replacing the freedom they had come to know - even for a short time - with a life confined to the chicken coop. The diabolical genius of it was that they still thought they were free. What his guides offered was the experience of engagement without the reality of freedom and it was a master stroke.

This degree of inter-realm cooperation was on an unprecedented level in modern history. To have this many physically visible spirit beings interacting on the earth was unheard of. Centuries ago, people had been much more aware of the spiritual realms and Moloch often reminisced about the times when he had been party to an overwhelming level of support - when the human desire to seek out and appease the Princes, Kings and Strongmen over principalities and nations was commonplace. The Ammonites were the last people to worship him with any degree of authority.

"How is it coming on, my boy?" Moloch spoke in to the silence to his subject. He had noticed a slight shift in this man and it made him uneasy. There was something undeniably ruthless about Nixon - a quality the god admired - but it seemed to be more and more directed at himself and this was an unacceptable turn of events. Moloch had been disappointed in the past by people who promised much but ultimately failed to deliver as they fell short at the final hurdle - usually as a consequence of greed or poor judgement. Peter Nixon had been different and did not seem to be susceptible to these weak traits. But that unpredictability also meant that Moloch found himself working with a man he could not read, could not manipulate and that, if he was completely honest with himself, alarmed him.

"You have nothing to concern yourself with, my Lord. All is as it should be," Nixon replied, with an obsequious smile.

"Remind me," Moloch pushed, trying to keep his voice even, "what are your next intentions?"

"Must we go over it again? I assure you, Master, we are well placed for a surge of support and following in September, when the schools go back. Do not concern yourself with the details, I have it in hand. Sit back and bask in what is coming - the glory days of a level of service you have not enjoyed for around twenty-five centuries."

Moloch bowed his head stiffly to proffer his consent, but he set his jaw with a steely determination. This man could not be allowed to side step him, he was on the alert.

Chapter 19: The Ammonite Abomination

Moloch had aspirations for power and domination which had never truly been realised. He refused to see himself as a second rate deity, consigned to history by biblical antagonists who had failed to portray him with the dignity and auspice he deserved. For centuries his advances had been overlooked and many did not even believe that the Order, where Nixon first encountered Moloch, still existed; never mind any comprehension about its driving spiritual force.

Moloch had enjoyed popularity throughout Phoenicia, Canaan and North Africa up to the fourth century BC, where he was relegated to mere demonhood by the followers of Yahweh. He hated the very mention of that name! He had drawn humans away from what had been a mutually beneficial arrangement - they fed his blood lust and Moloch granted them favour and protection. How he longed for the Halcyon days when parents would willingly come and offer their first born children to him in exchange for a good harvest or health, or wealth even. He had done his best to reciprocate, he was fair. The better the offering, the better the reward. It had been fine until the meddling Yahweists had destroyed the natural order of things, promising the people things that Moloch simply could not deliver.

Once they had an alternative, people started believing that they didn't need him anymore.

The Romans hadn't helped his cause. He had tried to revive interest in following his particular brand of religion amongst the Phoenician colonies at Carthage. But the Romans - who hated anyone different from themselves - managed to misinterpret Moloch's motives and misrepresent him all over again. They didn't understand the purity of an infant sacrifice, the latent power of the dedication of the first born and all the weight that carried in the realms of the kingdoms which Moloch frequented. There was nothing more potent, so why was he wrong to align himself with it? Or try to benefit from it? It was simple mathematics; no melodrama or sentiment need be applied. He regretted the reputation he had since gained for being a second rate fallen angel with little intelligence, who clamoured for battle but never won. He would not lose this one! He would not lose it to the Brightness, and he most certainly would not lose it to Nixon. He had dropped his guard, briefly, looked on the man as a worthy confederate and the man had responded with disdain. He would not be beaten again, the battle was on!

Chapter 20: The Waves

Xander had found his talk with Scarlett had settled his nerves somewhat and given him a new confidence and belief in what he was doing. He took some time to think about what she had said and to take what he could from the parallels which their experiences had thrown up. He was someone who liked to be organised and as such, was methodical in his thinking. There were names he had come across, more than once some of them, and he wanted to map out his knowledge somehow to see where the gaps were or to help him to focus on where to go next on this journey of discovery.

August had started, in much the same vein as July had finished - grim and grey. There was little enticement to be outside, or even to socialise with his friends, so Xander had spent most of his summer holidays confined to his house - more specifically, his room.

He reached out for his journal and flicked back through the pages with an air of nostalgia, hoping something would leap out at him and direct him. He missed the thrill of the Castle and the wonder of seeing longed for things come to pass. It got him thinking about Scarlett's first encounter with the Brightness and her commission to build a place for collective visualisation. It had sounded very much as if the Brightness had this in mind and was merely on the lookout for a partner. He was that partner now and he was desperate to know more about the entity he had worked with for nearly two years. When he had first seen it, he had mistaken it for an ethereal light, purely responding to the will and wishes of others. However, as time had passed, he recognised the ascendancy behind it and the pull of this compelling force that seemed to want to inspire a goodness and benevolence in people; to enlarge their dreams and feed their visions with limitless possibility.

"Where did you come from?" Xander inquired, aloud. He had succeeded in the past in communicating with the Brightness in this way. It seemed to be waiting for him to ask questions.

Quite unexpectedly, Xander found himself experiencing a gentle shaking. He was alarmed at first, wondering if it was an earthquake. But he soon realised that it was not the natural world around him that was manifesting this disturbance. He seemed to enter in to a tunnel of light which flickered before his eyes like rapidly turning pages. Along with it was a sensation not dissimilar to airplane turbulence. He did not resist the experience, but sank in to it and relaxed as he had learned to do with the Castle. The experience sharpened as he did this and he sensed the molecules of atmosphere around him with incredible clarity, feeling both his oneness with them and their corporate urging for him to travel this impossible path.

He relaxed further and felt an instant response from his surroundings. The flickering had given way to blue sky and fluffy white clouds, but he was not looking up at them, he was among them, perpetuating the sensation of flying. Xander was intoxicated by the exquisite feeling of being rolled around by waves of sympathetic and intuitively connected atmosphere. As he got used to it, it felt like surfing on the clouds and rolling waves of air. It was alive and responsive, playing with him it seemed, as the molecules passed him from one invisible wave to another with a gentleness that was awe inspiring but a firmness that carried weight and force. It was exciting, exhilarating and releasing. For the first time in his life, Xander knew what freedom was.

Chapter 21: The Vessel

At that moment, Xander would not have been disappointed to learn that this would be where he was to spend eternity. He had no concept of passing time here, whether it was the work of a moment or a thousand years did not even seem relevant. But as he looked out in to the expanse of sky, lying back on a cushion of air, he saw something materialise before him. It looked like something he had seen on the Antiques Roadshow during one of his father's 'Let's spend the evening as a family,' moments. He was momentarily distracted by a sudden swell of sadness which accompanied the thought. In spite of that meaning he might have to endure programmes he wouldn't normally watch, it was comforting to curl up together on the sofas and frankly it was way too long since they had done it. Xander dragged himself back to the present, determined not to let the nostalgia of lost experience cause him to lose his place here, where he believed he was on the brink of something both exciting and poignant.

What he saw was to all intents and purposes a Renaissance scent bottle made of glass and iridescent with peacock hues and radiant gold. It was breathtakingly beautiful, a jewel in itself. From above - although no point of origin could be determined - small droplets fell and crystallized like multi-faceted diamonds. Effortlessly they were collected in the vessel, each droplet catching the light from an equally indeterminate source and pulsating with this light like a living entity before being contained. As quickly as they had started, the droplets ceased to fall and the bottle itself imperceptibly altered its shape until it became a cupped hand. Xander marvelled at how such a transformation could take place when it was so extreme, yet it felt so rational. He continued to watch the metamorphosis unfold with undisguised wonder.

The individual gems had undergone a similar transformation and had taken on the appearance of a thick and viscous liquid in the hand, like a pool of coruscating light. Slowly the cupped hand gently rotated and began to pour out the liquid in a steady and eternal stream of water, which Xander watched, enthralled. As it fell through the atmosphere, the volume of the water seemed to increase and spread out, running down through numerous atmospheric layers. As it passed through a new layer, or realm, it took on a different colour and Xander was quick to recognise that with each passing seam, it reflected first one, then the next and the next, until all seven hues of the rainbow were represented. They fell and pulsated, not in the traditional arc one associates with a rainbow, but with the wonderful organic vibrations of the Northern Lights. It was breathtaking, seeing the individual colours expressed and then witnessing the corporate revelation of the perfect beauty they achieved. In addition to the visual spectacle, it was as if each layer seemed to emanate a different and separate identity, like a living thing, and he was in awe of the power he was beholding. However, the combined force of their union was intensifying with each passing moment, until he felt he might be overcome by the sheer intoxicating potency of it. Instinctively he knew that what he had just witnessed was the origin and source of the Brightness.

He looked down towards the Earth for the first time, almost surprised to see it there. He was instantly dismayed to see that, below the seven layers of glory, a dark film was stretched out, preventing the streams of iridescent water from raining down upon it. He knew as he looked at it, that the film was the darkness that had descended upon his nation under the dominion of Nixon. What horrified him more than that, was that it was not just his little country that sat under this cloud, but the whole Earth seemed to be affected by it. It was as if an agreement had been made of global proportions to shut out the Brightness. Surely he did not have to contend with all of this? England was a large enough arena for him to try to get his head around; this was overwhelming.

In response to his anxiety, a wave of peace came over him. "There are other Defenders of the Truth. This is not your battle alone. Do not be afraid, for fear paralyses." That voice again, who was that?

"Who are you? Where are you?" The disembodied form which Xander had taken, rotated so he could see in all directions on the horizontal plane. He felt like he was doing a space walk. Finally he looked up, but still he saw nothing.

"I am the Truth, Xander. You know when you hear me that this is who I am."

He did. "Where should I go now?"

"You need partners. They will come in different guises. Be careful who you trust."

As suddenly as it had began, the vision ended. Xander could hear the last sentence ringing in his ears. He thought of Scarlett; Rosie, Dan and Lucie for starters. He trusted them. Perhaps the time had come to share his burden with a wider audience.

Chapter 22: Old Friends

Xander did not rush immediately to engage his friends - this was not a time for knee-jerk reactions. He carefully considered his history with them, remembering the warning to be careful who he trusted. Scarlett was a given and he felt, although a time would come to reconnect with her, it was not now. Rosie he trusted implicitly. There was absolutely no artifice about her. They had been together on this since day one and had developed a strong bond of friendship and mutual respect. If there was anything, where Rosie was concerned, it was that she lacked a little self-confidence, not quite believing in the validity of her own contributions to the cause. Dan was someone Scarlett had introduced him to, but that was right at the start, before any of the sinister developments had taken place. He had not had as much to do with him as he had with Rosie - mainly because they didn't go to the same school, so a lot of their collaboration had been in the Castle itself - but he had no qualms about trusting him. Dan was a solid character who brought a freshness and directness to proceedings and Xander both liked and trusted him. Dan was in.

Xander shifted his position as his thoughts turned from people in his immediate locality to those he had met through the Castle who were further afield. The most obvious choice was Lucie. He was sure she was on the up and up; she had been the one to blow the lid off Nixon's scheme to be fair, and anyway, he liked her. Lucie may be vulnerable on one level and possessed an ability to become almost invisible due to the emotional baggage she carried with her, but on the other hand, she was brave and feisty and did not tolerate anything which smacked of injustice. Xander admired her gritty determination to carry on where others might have crumpled, and ability to not bow to the pressure of failure. She made no excuses for herself and that impressed him. Nixon had used her, in the worst possible way, exploiting her grief and love for her dead mother to manipulate her in to working for him. As soon as she realised what he was doing, she had tried to make amends for her part in things by unfailing service to Scarlett and the cause. She wasn't local though, which made things more difficult. In the Castle geography was irrelevant, but here and now, until something else opened up for them, it was unavoidable. Xander decided to wait a while where Lucie was concerned and focus on Rosie and Dan for now.

The morning after his last supernatural encounter, Xander went through his routines with measured focus before drawing out his phone to contact his friends. Text or call? He looked at the screen as it sprang to life and selected his contacts list. He scrolled down to Rosie first and her picture popped up, smiling and shy. He remembered taking the photograph during a cover lesson last summer and it captured her perfectly. He smiled. Call.

Xander selected her number and it rang.

It kept ringing. He was just preparing for the voicemail to kick in when she answered.

"Hello." She sounded distant and it took him aback.

"Rosie?"

"Yes. What do you want, Xander?"

"I was hoping we could meet up. I've got loads to tell you."

There was a pause. "It's been a while. Why now?"

"What do you mean?" he asked. He wasn't used to this side of Rosie's character. She sounded hurt.

"I haven't been avoiding you, I just needed some time."

"Well it felt like it. I thought you wanted us to work together? You went to see Scarlett then I didn't hear from you. I assumed you didn't think I was up to it!"

"No! That's not it at all!" Xander hurriedly explained. "It's been a strange time and I didn't know how to describe it to myself, let alone anyone else! I'm sorry. I thought I'd see if Dan was free too," Xander ventured, hoping to pacify her.

"He's a bit miffed he hasn't heard from you either," Rosie said, blandly. She obviously still hadn't forgiven him.

"Have you spoken to him?"

"We've been in touch, yes. It's not just about you, you know."

"I'm sorry, Rosie, really I am. I didn't mean to cut you both out, I just needed to work through some stuff," Xander tried to reassure her. "Can we meet? The three of us? Please?"

"Ok. You'll have to call Dan though and get back to me with a time. I'm free all day." Then she hung up.

Xander was stunned. He had no idea he had hurt her, he'd been so wrapped up in his own thing. He felt a prickle of indignation as he tried to justify his actions to himself, but he knew she had a point and he was angry with himself for letting it happen. It was with less optimism that he phoned Dan. He received a cool response at first, but curiosity got the better of his friend and the time and the place was set.

Chapter 23: The War Room

Xander was surprised to find that he had butterflies. He had checked the time on his watch, his phone, the microwave and his alarm clock as he had advanced nervously around the house waiting for his friends to arrive. They had arranged to meet at his house at two o'clock, and whichever clock he looked at seemed to be conspiring with all the others to run slowly. It was an inauspicious place for a strategy meeting of this magnitude, but it was convenient as both of his parents were out, down at the restaurant. It had become a millstone around his father's neck as he hadn't finished paying off his loan when the recession had struck. The hospitality industry had been hit hard and he was struggling to keep up with the payments. There was nothing Xander could do at the moment and he felt helpless. But one of his motivations for destroying Nixon was to get his dad back on his feet. He knew this was the right thing for his dad, but he had been robbed of much of the pleasure of it by the current circumstances. There was no point in feeling responsible or guilty for how things had turned out, regrets solved nothing. As he reflected on this, Xander felt a gritty determination settle in between his shoulder blades and into his back. He instinctively straightened up and mustered a resolve that drove the butterflies out of his stomach with a clear message not to return. They may be kids;

this might be his front room; but this most certainly was war.

At that moment the doorbell rang. Rosie and Dan stood on the front step together and Xander briefly considered the possibility that they had engineered it this way so neither of them had to arrive alone. He pushed the thought out of his mind; this was no time for insecurity. He realised how pleased he was to see them and smiled broadly as he welcomed them in.

"Hey guys! It is **so** good to see you!"

"Alright mate?" Dan was reassuringly Dan, and any fears Xander may have had of having blown their friendship melted away. Rosie, on the other hand, said nothing. She smiled at him as she walked in, but her eyes registered a vulnerability that told him of her hurt. He had aggrieved her, he knew it, but seeing her face to face, reading it in her eyes made him feel rotten.

"It's good to see you Rosie. Really good," he spoke in a low voice, hoping she would let his words in. She was the closest he had to a sibling and the thought of losing that relationship shredded his heart.

"You too," she murmured back. "I've missed you." As she turned to him, he read her forgiveness in her countenance, but could see the caveat that came with it as clearly as if she had spoken it out, 'Don't do it again!'

They stood together in the hall for a moment enveloped in an awkward silence. Dan was looking from one to the other of them with an expression that suggested he had just missed the punch line of an amusing joke.

"Everything ok between you two?" he asked, just about resisting the urge to add a knowing wink.

"Yeah, fine," Rosie added, convincingly, pushing past them both and heading in to the front room. "Are we going to get started then?"

Dan looked at Xander and raised an eyebrow, inviting his friend to comment. Xander just shrugged and smiled, "You heard the woman!" They both laughed and followed Rosie in.

Social niceties were far from everyone's thoughts and Xander, particularly, was keen to see if either of his friends had had any supernatural encounters similar to his own. Neither of them could attest to anything specific, but they had both had dreams of angelic beings communicating with them and reassuring them on some sub-atomic level. Rosie had been wary of this after being so nearly taken in by Naamah, one of Nixon's guides, back at the Castle. But Dan reassured her that the entity he had encountered had felt different and that there would be beings that they could trust.

Xander did not know until he started talking, how much he was going to share with his friends. But it turned out to be everything and he was glad of the opportunity to unburden himself with what he had been carrying.

"I'm not imagining it, am I?" he asked finally, when he had finished his recount of events over the last six weeks. He knew he was not, but somehow he wanted to hear them agree with him, that this was not going to change how they saw him.

"I don't think so," Rosie reassured him. "There was always something about you; an authority, an aptitude, I don't know how to describe it. Whatever this is we are fighting here Xander, you are part of the solution."

"We all are, surely?" he quickly responded, keen to maintain their Musketeer dynamics.

"Of course we are, mate. But you have the keys." Dan looked at him solemnly. "We are with you on this, aren't we Rosie?" he looked over at her questioningly and she vigorously nodded her agreement. "But I believe there will be times when you will need to take the lead. The Brightness has chosen you - just look at what you have experienced over the last few weeks - and I for one have no problem seeing why."

"Thanks Dan, I appreciate that. It's been a lonely and confusing time, I have to admit. But at last I feel like we have somewhere to start. How do you feel about a collective attempt to visit Olam?" There was a twinkle in Xander's eye and they all felt the rollercoaster sensation that accompanies excitement and adventure.

"No guts, no glory!" Dan stated and they all laughed.

Chapter 24: Permission

Peter Nixon left nothing to chance. He looked down at the paperwork in front of him. It was the document that was about to be couriered to every secondary school in the country. He looked at the cover page and smiled at it proudly, tapping it with his right fore-finger. 'Guidelines and Protocol for the Implementation of the Collective.' His eyes scanned the title and his mind momentarily drifted off in to the near future, when this very document would ensure his prospective position as the nation's leader, and satisfy Moloch at the same time. He mused at the mutual exclusivity of these two scenarios and realised that he no longer felt dependent on the beast for his own success.

To the untrained eye he was alone in his office, but to those whose eyes had been opened to the realms beyond the natural, it was full of supernatural beings. Still they chose to present themselves as beings of light - although beneath that barely disguised façade was a broiling mass of depravity, mistrust and evil intent. As usual, Shapeshifter and Naamah, Nixon's most trusted guides, flanked him left and right.

"When this goes out from here," he spoke aloud, addressing the room and its sinister occupants, "it will be your responsibility to see that my wishes are implemented to the full. You each have a room in this realm from which to operate and you can be fully visible in your guise as light-bearers. I want people to see you, believe in you and follow you as though it were the most natural thing in the world." Nixon reached for the document on his desk and held it aloft. "But the first thing you must push for, the crucial element here, is permission. You must get as many parents as possible to sign the contract which gives us access to their children. Our Master, Moloch, requires this offering and it is your job to ensure that every parent is given the opportunity to sign over their children. Of course, they will think they are securing their future and giving them the opportunity to be part of a national movement that will benefit them, keep them safe. And it will, we will make sure of that. But there is a potency in their agreement which will not be understood by them, but is everything to us. Once that agreement starts to flow in and feed Moloch, our power will also increase and our influence in the realms around us after that. I am not just looking for domination over a nation here, we have the chance to eliminate the Brightness and its influence once and for all, and for that I need the children. Do not fail me."

The beings in the room bowed before Nixon and it took him back to a time in the Castle when he had seen himself being worshipped. At last, his destiny was being fulfilled.

Chapter 25: Ma'on

Ma'on was a place that existed on one of the seven spiritual planes which Xander had witnessed in his vision of the Brightness. It was the yellow realm and was bathed in a glorious golden light at all times. Usually this place was untainted by the sickness which had invaded the natural realm. It had succeeded in maintaining an uninterrupted level of peace and security since time immemorial. But there was a disturbance here now. The beings which inhabited it - ministering angels whose job it was to oversee the Earth and those on it; to connect with them and draw out their spirituality - had sensed a darkness. Ripples had gone through their realm which interfered with the very fabric of it, like a glitch in the space/time continuum.

Tzadok called a meeting. He was the High Priest of Ma'on and had walked, uninterrupted, through its gardens for countless centuries. Of course, he had witnessed times in history where the Earth itself had been overshadowed by darkness, but the pendulum had always swung back. This was different. The darkness was spreading. It had moved through the layers, pushing the Brightness back and extinguishing the lights of violet, indigo, green and blue and now it was poised to savage Ma'on and destroy its beauty and tranquillity. Tzadok was troubled. Legends foretold of a time such as this, but he was still unprepared for the inky fingers of evil which picked away at the edges of the kingdom he loved and threatened the guardians within.

The gathering was a beautiful sight. The ministering angels carried an innate light that glowed with such purity it was dazzling. As they came together an involuntary song rose up between them which carried on the air and pulsated with clarity and unity. Tzadok paused before speaking, almost overwhelmed by what he beheld. It had only been necessary on three occasions since he had walked this realm to gather in this way. The union created had been enough then to push back the darkness and send it fleeing in the opposite direction. But he sensed the shift; this was different and it unsettled him.

"My friends," he addressed the crowd that stretched out in all directions like a throbbing wave of light. His voice became part of the song and carried, effortlessly off, in to the distance. "We have a challenge of unrivalled proportions. An agreement has taken place on the Earth with Machon and an evil has been released. Moloch sits on the throne there. He has been defeated before, but this is unprecedented. There is a man who has learnt the ways of Machon and has become a spearhead, piercing through our realms with accuracy and devastating success. It has always been our commission to wait to be engaged by the people of the Earth, then to encourage them and minister in love to their spirits. I do not need to tell you your grave undertaking. But a time has come for us to act, to search out the fire carriers and teach them how to battle this. Take them to Olam and show them the ancient ways. There is not much time."

The words he spoke reverberated around the company of angels and a gradual transformation was taking place among them. Their wings, which had previously not been visible beneath their white robes, began to flex and beat, creating first a gentle breeze, then an ever increasing wind. A fragrance carried on the wind like a pheromone, which seemed to ignite a deep conviction within each one of them. They grew in stature; their faces took on an attitude of determination; and their robes became glowing armour which took on the radiant hue of their golden realm and shone so brightly that the combined effect was like looking at the sun. The darkness, which was ebbing around the perimeter of the realm like a toxic tide, retreated somewhat. But they knew it would not last. Time was of the essence. As one awesome force, the angels rose and, like fiery comets, set off in all directions to scour the Earth for the fire carriers - the ones with a calling to engage with the coming conflict.

Chapter 26: A Different Level

Rosie, Dan and Xander sat together in the living room feeling a little awkward. It was not that they were unfamiliar with collective visualisation, but it felt different trying to push through on their own, without either the labyrinths of the Castle or the reassuring guidance of Scarlett Tang. It was like a rite of passage, a pivotal moment upon which they could not fail.

"How should we do this then?" Rosie asked. It may have looked like she was taking charge of the situation, but in actual fact she was asking the question to deflect the need to come up with a solution away from herself and on to one of the boys. She was feeling a little apprehensive about the possibility of encountering some of the things which Xander had described; although this was definitely mixed in equal measure with an excitement at the prospect.

"It might sound weird, but I've just spoken to it before. It hasn't always worked, to be fair, but Adon Olam did say to me that I could speak to things and cause them to happen, so shall we just agree now to try this together?" He looked around the familiar room at his friends, feeling strangely calm and relaxed.

Without realising it, Xander had hit upon a vital concept; agreement. There is such power in it, and as the three of them bowed their heads to begin a different level of visualisation - one without the safe confines of the Castle, where they had learnt to flex their spiritual muscles and spread their wings of potential - a tangible atmosphere of peace and power descended upon the room.

"Brightness," Xander addressed the entity they had all come to love. "We are here to learn more about Olam. We want to walk in the ancient ways and partner with the Truth. We want to see Nixon and all that he stands for defeated and pushed back so you can once again influence our nation. We want to do this together. Take us where you had in mind when you first called us to follow you along this path of discovery."

In that moment, three sixteen year old children believed with all their being that they had reached a turning point in their lives and in the destiny which lay ahead for their nation, and that things would never be the same again.

They were right.

Chapter 27: The Walk

Suddenly they found themselves on a paved road. It led off in to the distance straight and true. They looked at each other in wonder, realising they had been successful in travelling together to this other-worldly place. For Xander, particularly, who had been here before, he was amazed to see his friends in front of him in physical form.

"What's that on your chest, Xander? And you Dan?" Rosie asked, curiously reaching out towards them.

The boys looked down simultaneously and Xander saw a small, bluish-white flame dancing playfully over his heart. He was puzzled. Had it always been there in this realm, he just hadn't been able to see it on himself? Rosie had one too, he noticed. His seemed to burn a little bigger and brighter than theirs, but they all had one.

"I don't know," he answered. "I've never noticed it before. But then I've always been on my own and I've not had much sense of my physical self always, as I've been so absorbed by my surroundings." He reached his finger round, as though he were about to prod a butterfly but was afraid of scaring it. He nudged the flame and it danced all the more. It made them laugh with a childlike enjoyment.

"Where are we?" asked Dan, the first one to tire of their game and really look around the place they had come to.

"It looks like Olam," Xander responded, "although I've only been here on a couple of occasions, it's been different every time. One thing it does seem to be consistently about though is roads, paths and streams."

"What should we do now?" Rosie looked about her like a foreigner in a strange land. The road they were on was all that was visible to them. Either side of it, the ground fell away in to a misty haze, like they were somehow trapped in a video game where the only reality was the thing they must focus on; the path.

"Let's walk, see where it takes us," Xander ventured. In front of them, the road stretched out to meet the distant horizon with no indication as to where it led, or from whence it had come. They walked.

Time had no place here, just as with Xander's other encounters, and they followed the road with no sense of the passage of it. The scenery did not change at all and nothing about the path itself altered either - its trajectory, its makeup, its gradient. Xander was just starting to wonder if the whole journey was going to turn out to be a fruitless waste of time, when he became aware that someone else seemed to have joined their select party. It was a gradual sense of another being among them, just as one might progressively become aware of being followed. He turned round, realised his suspicion had been correct and stopped walking. Dan and Rosie instinctively stopped as well, even before they were aware of the reason why. They followed Xander's gaze to a couple of feet behind them on the path and were quite startled to behold the man who stood there, not having divined the presence of anyone along with them. He was tall and ethereal. His face seemed to hold in its expression a thousand years of wisdom.

"Hello," Xander welcomed, bowing slightly and a little awkwardly, as he was unsure of the correct protocol for greeting such beings. "Who are you?" he added, emboldened.

"I am Ethan. I have been sent out to search for the fire carriers. We have work to do."

"Do you mean us?" Rosie inquired. "Are there more people here? We haven't seen anyone else." She was keen to engage the man and gain some insight as to what this particular experience was all about. They had already determined that none of these encounters were for mere entertainment or fancy; there was something to be learnt, something to be gained, something to be experienced and she was eager that they establish that particular fact as early on in the occurrence as possible.

"This is **your** path, you will not see anyone else on it. But look," he motioned for them to survey their surroundings, casting his arm out in a wide, sweeping arch. As he did so, it was as if a veil was drawn back and the mist which had masked all but the path before them receded, melting away until they could see many, many roads winding, crossing, stretching out. Some of them had small groups or individuals upon them and each one, as far as they could discern, carried a blue flame over their heart.

Initially Xander was excited by what he saw. The relief that others were travelling in this realm was reassuring. However, the number of roads he could see was virtually limitless and less than half of them, he calculated, had anyone upon them.

"Is that all?" he asked, trying not to sound disheartened. "Is this a representation of the people of the world who are engaged with the same battle, or is this just our nation?"

Ethan was silent for a moment, reflective. He looked out at the ancient pathways with a fondness that spoke of centuries of commitment. "This, my friends, is a timeless place. These are all the people, in all of the world, in all of time, who have found their way on to these roads. This is not an easy place to locate. You do not stumble upon Olam, you search it out and simultaneously, it reaches out to you. You are not here by accident. You are here to engage with the battle for the Earth."

"Will you show us?" It was Dan, he had been quiet up to now. Xander turned to look at him. Dan was very laid back. Xander had built a good friendship with him over the last couple of years, but he had always questioned how seriously Dan took things. He was a hard person to read as you were never quite sure if he was along for the ride, having found himself caught up in all of this by some kind of miraculous twist of fate, and now he was forced to go along with it because the merry-go-round was moving and it was too late to get off. But, in this moment, looking at his friend Xander could see a fierce resolve and a determination to take this on, whatever the cost. His eyes spoke of his dedication and Xander felt guilty for ever allowing himself to question whether or not Dan was as committed as he was. He smiled at him and the three of them intuitively reached for each other's hands and stood together.

Tzadok looked down from his vantage point at the three young people, united in their fight. He had felt like Xander, that the travellers on the roads were scanty to say the least, but this sign of solidarity warmed his heart. The flames they carried seemed to burn brighter as a result and the High Priest allowed himself to believe that this battle could still be won.

Chapter 28: Machon

Most of the realms that existed around the Earth were places of safety and light. The Brightness was the force which connected them together. What Xander had witnessed in his previous vision were the seven different realms of light. Each one had an independent identity and colour. The colours themselves were significant, influencing the Earth with their particular identities. The yellow band of Ma'on was where the Brightness was most at home and this had become the front line against the advancing darkness. Machon was unlike the other realms, in that it was the dwelling place of darkness and did not have a designated territory. It was continually moving, reaching and retreating, absorbing other realms wherever it could. It had never succeeded in defeating Ma'on, but for the first time ever, it had been able to penetrate it. This was solely due to the creation of the Castle.

As far as the Overseer and Tzadok were concerned, the Castle had been a gamble. Knowing that time was short, a link had been forged of unprecedented proportions in order to allow access to the spiritual planes. With the unique partnership which existed between Scarlett and the Brightness, what had taken the spiritual pioneers and the ancient mystics decades to achieve, she had been allowed to access in a matter of a few short years and her followers had been able to achieve in minutes. This acceleration was for two reasons: the access points had been cleared by those who had gone before, in much the same way as a gardener clears the weeds away to make the land fertile and useable for those that want to plant it; also, there was a pressing need to take things to the next level. Evil was advancing and becoming more subtle as it evolved to change hearts and captivate minds. Time was of the essence.

Nixon did not care for the intricacies of the spirit realms - just like a lottery winner doesn't care how his supercar works; only that it goes fast, delivers the power he craves and provides him with the necessary buzz. He had a plan, he had harnessed the power and now he assumed the forces he worked with would respond to his vision and fill in the gaps, the way oil instinctively runs over the ground and finds its way into the cracks and crevices to create a smooth surface and occupy everything it touches.

Moloch drove the forces of darkness and it was his responsibility - as far as Nixon was concerned - to make sure everyone else performed in accordance with the plan. He knew that what was required to ensure their success was a convincing infiltration of the enemy forces; deception and subterfuge were their eternal weapons. He knew the Brightness was still operational, but he did not know what their strategy was. He had been outwitted before by these guardians of virtue and was therefore not as blasé as Nixon about the certainty of their success. The angels of Ma'on had been commissioned, they had seen the burst of light like a nuclear explosion. What they had been commissioned to do, however, he was yet to discover. Moloch no longer sat as easily on his throne, he was determined to find a way to defeat the Brightness, once and for all.

Chapter 29: The Seven

The three young people had been told by Ethan that they needed to walk along the path until they came upon Adon Olam. "He will tell you about the realms you have been called to."

"Who is Adon Olam?" Rosie had asked. She knew Xander had met him on a couple of occasions, but she did not know who he actually was. The whole thing still sounded very mysterious and vague to her.

"He is the Overseer. He has been charged with ensuring that the realms are in balance. The Brightness depends upon their harmony."

"But, if some of the realms have already been consumed by the darkness," Xander had asked, puzzled by what he had seen in his vision, "then is the Brightness compromised?"

"I cannot answer your questions, but the Overseer can. Look to him." And Ethan was gone.

They walked on and on with no sign of anyone. "This is pointless," Dan complained, "there's nothing here." He sat down on the road, despondent.

"Maybe we are not actually seeking him," Xander responded slowly, thinking out loud.

"What do you mean?" Rosie asked, encouragingly, sensing he was on to something.

"I'm still new to this, but when I ask specifically for something, that seems to be when I have the most success. Shall we focus on him, like a visualisation?" Xander felt this was the key to meeting their guide and his renewed enthusiasm encouraged Dan, who stood up nodding.

"Do you want to say something, Xander? This place seems to respond to you."

It seemed strange to be visualising within a visualisation, but the fact that being here in Olam felt as real as being on the Earth somehow diluted the incongruity of it.

"Ok," he replied, shyly. "Adon Olam. We have come to be taught by you. Please show us the way." Xander realised he had closed his eyes as he spoke - probably a self-preservation tactic, to stop him from feeling too self-conscious - so he opened them again expectantly. Nothing seemed to have changed and he fought the mild disappointment which had caused both his head and his expression to fall. It was Rosie who saw it first; the figure walking towards them out of the haze on the road ahead.

"Look!" she exclaimed.

They walked towards it, approaching what they now saw to be a man, with supernatural speed. He stopped and nodded his head in a respectful greeting.

Adon Olam did not look like an angel, he looked like a man. Seeing him again, reminded Xander that he hadn't actually described him to his friends, or really discerned the ordinary nature of his appearance. There was something entirely forgettable, yet remarkably arresting about him all at once. His age was indeterminate - like a history teacher - giving off the aura of an old man in aspect and wisdom, yet having eyes which reflected the joyful, carefree demeanour of youth. His countenance was serious, yet playful. He was a dichotomy. In terms of his build, he was neither tall nor was he stocky, but his presence was charged with authority and power. The Overseer was a good title for him, as the children immediately felt there was nothing going on that he did not know about or allow.

"Shall we begin?" Xander had witnessed before how he seemed to speak without moving his lips and he knew by looking at his friends that they had heard him too.

"What you have seen concerns the past and the future. You need to be shown the ways of the Seven before time runs out. I will send you a teacher from each realm. It is vital that you understand what they carry as the Brightness depends upon them all. You have seen the colours, in the Castle, so you have already encountered the seven spirits that combine together to enhance the Brightness. Their positions are under threat because the darkness has a counterfeit in place. You will be taught to carry their identities until you become channels for the Breakout. Without it, there can be no victory. Watch, be on your guard and beware of the counterfeit. Time is short and the window of opportunity becomes ever smaller. You carry the heart," he pointed to Rosie, "you carry the faith," he pointed to Dan, "and you carry the vision." Xander felt a surge of electricity pass through him as Adon Olam pointed at him. "A cord of three is not easily broken." Then he was gone and so was the ancient way. They were back in Xander's living room, stunned in to silence.

Chapter 30: Business as Usual

Moloch was in the Castle. He liked it here - it had taken him centuries to gain access to this realm so he spent as much of his time as he could here. He did not see his permanent enthronement as a weakness, he had no desire to roam around. There was power in his position; others came to him, knelt before him, worshipped him. He saw no need to pursue anyone, walk anywhere or even raise himself from the throne which shouted out his sovereignty. Walking among the people was a sign of weakness, why should he debase himself thus? No, let the people come to him. And they did. Well, Nixon did. There was no point in advertising his authority here and risk losing support. The system they had in place worked well: the children - and indeed adults of Nixon's choosing - came to the Castle as often as they desired and accessed the rooms just as they always had. A purpose built throne room existed for Moloch and the guides moved to and fro between him and the Collective.

They had not really discussed the long term role of the Castle. Once the new order was established, then the Castle could well become obsolete, as children could access the spirit realm at any time by connecting with the guides which would be fully visible at all times on the Earth. Moloch liked the idea that Nixon, or anyone else who chose to still make the 'trip' here, could find him in his throne room and bow down. But things were set to change, the beast knew that, and he looked around him already feeling a twinge of nostalgia for the heady days of the Castle. He did not have such a clear sense of what was to come as Nixon seemed to and this made him uneasy - sharing someone else's vision meant he risked the possibility of being demoted somewhere down the line and he knew that the man was capable of this kind of treachery. He needed watching; everyone needed watching. Paranoia exists where peace does not and peace was never something Moloch had sought out or experienced for himself. He preferred the cut and thrust of battle and deceit, but he had to admit that being on the receiving end of it was not an enviable position.

The atmosphere as well as the operational procedures were a far cry from the original vision which Scarlett had sought to deliver. Initially, when Nixon had assumed leadership, the children had continued to follow their desire to see social transformation and thereby preserved the observance of bringing their naive requests with them to the Castle. Scarlett may have encouraged such folly, but the new order did not tolerate it. The Castle was no longer to be a place where people could come with a vision and seek the fulfilment of it; it was to be a place where a system was predetermined and you merely engaged with it, feeding its power and influence by allowing it to channel your own life blood and essence. As juxtaposed as this concept was, the shift itself needed to be a subtle one, so as not to raise suspicion. This was achieved through a gradual process of first allowing the children to present their requests, but absorbing them rather than channelling them. The disappointing results of the Castle under the cloud had done much to accelerate the lack of expectation, so it was in relatively no time at all that hopes waned about seeing results. But rather than experiencing sensations of disappointment or a lack of hope that one might feel when faced with the reality of their lack of progress, what the guides did so well was to distract the children from noticing the actual results by making themselves - in their guise as captivating creatures of light - the focal point of the engagement. So gradually, the children came, not to visualise for change as they had been accustomed to do in the past, but to engage with the 'angelic' beings, who in turn drew out their desires and conveyed their wishes as an offering of purity to feed the diabolical Moloch. To put it bluntly, the guides were literally sucking the life out of the children and their visualisations, or their hopes. As a consequence, Moloch's power was on the ascendancy, as was that of the guides, until they were able to subtly alter the exchanges that were taking place in this realm. They had now reached the point where, rather than just absorb the visualisations and transfer them to gratify and augment Moloch, they were now able to create a counter-flow which acted like a virus in the recipient. The dormancy of this infection was what Nixon was relying on for the long-term success of his plan. Like planting a trigger in an army of robots, which could one day be activated with devastating results.

It was, as far as the children were concerned, a much more passive arrangement than before. It was not that they took on the evil in any physical way and manifested it - that would have been a dangerous scheme and raised the alarm in parents and teachers about the potential dangers of the programme. Nixon's request was that they sow a seed of allegiance to him. Moloch had challenged him at the time this was proposed, fearful that Peter Nixon was trying to override him and become the object of worship himself. Calmly and cunningly, his protégée assured him that this was the safest way. The parents believed in him and had built a pedestal for him; the children knew him and trusted him already; the saintly Scarlett Tang had given him her wholehearted endorsement - well Shapeshifter had, and that was the same thing. Introducing Moloch now would muddy the waters. Reluctantly, the demon king had been persuaded and agreed and the man was one step closer to his goal.

The plan was progressing nicely. Peter knew that essentially they were treading water over the summer, but he was wise enough not to rush things. People kept coming, that was what was important, and they enjoyed the stability of the Castle. By September, they would be in a position to move the whole operation to the Earthly realm and the expansion he could see as a result was exponential. Not only would he have a guide in every school, he planned on having a tiered system of communicants to increase the numbers who would channel his vision and be bound in to his Empire. His star was ascending and he could see no obstacle in his path.

Chapter 31: A Little Bit of Narnia in London

The three friends had been back in the natural realm for quite a while, but as yet no one had found any relevant words to speak in to the silence which ensued. Eye contact was something else they avoided as they sat on the sofas in Xander's living room. It was a bright, comfortable and homely space which offered them a reassuring reference to normality after the alien environment they had inhabited moments before. They drew comfort from it and reset their internal compasses, which had been spinning wildly since their return and were only now settling to find north, and balance, and calm. Xander was sitting alone on the two seater sofa which faced the window and found himself staring at the glass at some passersby. Although the house was only a couple of feet from the pavement, they had chosen not to mask the view with nets or blinds, and he was more grateful of this than ever before as he found it settling to watch normal people doing normal things, but it also reminded him that they had a responsibility which far outweighed their own needs or proclivities. For whatever reason, they were in the middle of some kind of battle taking place in the unseen realms which directly impacted the Earth. The angelic forces were gathering, but they needed people to partner with. Wistfully, Xander thought back to stories his mother had read him as a youngster. He had loved

C. S. Lewis's imaginative tales of battles over the Earth and had longed to experience Narnia or Middle Earth for himself. Incredibly, it seemed that his dreams were coming true!

Finally Xander glanced across at his friends who had been similarly deep in thought. Rosie was staring at the fireplace with a fixed expression that seemed to be taking in nothing in particular. Her legs were drawn up under her to her left and she was absent-mindedly rubbing her toes. Dan had stretched himself out and was resting his head on the back of the sofa. He looked like a sturdy plank leaning against it with his body completely straight, as though someone had propped him up there for a moment but forgotten about him. His eyes were closed and, apart from being able to detect the gentle rise and fall of his chest as he breathed, he was motionless.

Not knowing how to begin, Xander cleared his throat. The others stirred and looked at him; he detected a hint of relief in their expressions, that he had taken charge somehow.

"We need to formulate some kind of plan to approach this, don't we?"

Dan nodded. "Do you think we all need to meet the Seven, or will they train us up individually so we can share the knowledge?"

"That's a good point. I suppose it depends on time, but it makes sense for us to take on two each at least, then feed back. What do you think Rosie?" Xander looked at her, trying to draw her in to the conversation.

"I agree. Do we all travel there together though, like we did today? Or do we go in our own time?"

"Let's see what we can accomplish individually over the next couple of days, then meet up again; say . . . . on Saturday?"

It was Wednesday now and on Saturday both of Xander's parents were scheduled to work at the restaurant, so it would give them privacy.

"Sounds good, mate," Dan concurred, nodding.

"Elevenish?"

"Yeah, I can do that," Rosie agreed.

It was arranged. There was nothing more to be done, so they went their separate ways.

Chapter 32: Truth

As it happened, Rosie was the first one to make it back. It was Thursday morning and she had been awake since about half past five - it may be overcast and murky, but it was still light early and the twins seemed to like waking up as soon as the grey dawn broke, so as not to miss a single sensory encounter for the day. There was nowhere quiet to go in her house as school was over for the summer for her younger sisters and a lot of the groups that her mum took the twins to didn't seem to be running through the holidays either. Sharing a room with the other girls meant she had nowhere private to relax and access the realms from home. She had been thinking about how to get around this problem and, last night, before she had fallen asleep, she had come up with a plan.

"Can I go and stay with Gran for a couple of days?" She built up the courage to ask the question at breakfast, not knowing what response it would get. Her mum had come to rely upon Rosie quite heavily for help around the house, especially since she had done her exams, and she looked up at Rosie from where she was wiping a flannel round her brothers' porridgey faces.

"Why do you want to do that?" she asked.

"I just want a bit of time to myself."

"In that case, can I come too?" her mum replied a little too quickly, and with a hint of irritation. Rosie couldn't tell if she was joking or cross because of the mixed signal and felt defensive herself. She loved her family, but she hadn't chosen any of this, why should she be chained to it? Immediately she felt guilty, watching her mum rushing around, getting the twins out of their high chairs, stuffing clothes in to the washing machine, breaking up a dispute over a toy tractor and trying to get her sisters to help clear the table. Rosie watched in silence, her breakfast untouched as she had suddenly lost her appetite.

"Give her a ring and see." Rosie looked up as the telephone was thrust in to her field of vision, taking her completely by surprise. Her mum was smiling kindly at her, as though she too had gone through the same range of emotions as Rosie, from belligerence to guilt to gentle compassion. Rosie smiled back appreciatively.

"Thanks Mum."

* * * * *

Two hours later she was on the tube heading west with a small rucksack of necessaries. Some of the time she would have to be sociable, she realised, inwardly coaching herself, but Gran knew how hectic things were at home and was happy to offer her a little respite. Every so often, excitement surged up within her at the prospect of this precious opportunity and more than once she caught a glimpse of her slightly distorted reflection in the train window with a definite grin on her face. She looked down at her lap, self-consciously, pretending to read the book which still lay open at page 137.

It was after lunch before Rosie felt she could ask to go to her room to 'read'. Gran often had a little nap in the afternoon, so it was perfect. She closed the door, feeling faintly awkward, like she was about to do something illegal. She looked at the neat little room reserved for grandchildren. It was rather dated, but that made her smile. There were ghosts of memory in the narrow bed with the dark wooden headboard, and the duvet cover with bunny rabbits on which she had loved when she was younger. A colourful crocheted blanket was neatly folded along the end of the bed and Rosie reached for it and pressed it up to her face between her clasped hands. She sat down on the bed, vividly recalling the first time she had stayed here without her parents, when she was five or six. Gran had put a night light in the room which she had found at a car boot sale, so she wouldn't feel scared. She glanced over at it standing on the tall boy on top of a lace doily, its brown sixties cable reaching down to the plug point below. It was rather tacky, she noticed now; a china tree with a family of squirrels living in it. The light shone from the small windows which had been cut out of the trunk. She remembered creating a whole back story for the family and giving them all names. She smiled again and breathed deeply, laying the blanket down and shuffling back so her feet left the floor and her back rested against the Laura Ashley floral wallpaper.

Rosie used the visualisation techniques that Scarlett had taught her to calm herself and picture where she wanted to be. She decided to go back to Olam and see who was there - if it was Adon Olam himself, he would undoubtedly have some wise words for her; or if it was one of the Seven, whoever they were, then her education would begin.

In no time at all, she was standing on a road in Olam. It felt wilder and lonelier and more austere being here on her own and she shivered.

"Are you cold?"

Rosie spun around, startled by the voice behind her. She saw a beautiful being who looked neither male nor female, but seemed to capture the gender qualities of both. A red glow appeared to emanate from him/her.

"Who are you?" Rosie asked, unimaginatively.

"I am the Spirit of Truth. You did the right thing coming here Rosie. I have some instructions for you which you are to communicate to your friends. There is no time to lose."

Chapter 33: Feedback

Rosie's heart was racing when she returned to the familiar room at her Gran's. She immediately reached for a notepad and wrote down all she could remember. The spirit being had spoken to her for only a few minutes, but it had felt like somewhere in her innermost being, a place inside herself that she had only just seen but in a moment knew that it was more **her** than any other version of herself she had come to know or present; that in that slice of time up there in the spirit realm she had connected with centuries of wisdom and experience. It was probably the most powerful and life altering situation she had ever encountered - and that was saying something after some of the things she had witnessed in the Castle. But this was different; it was no longer an external experience - exciting as that had been - it was a core-rocking, deep, deep exchange which grounded itself in her foundational identity.

She closed her eyes and felt the peace and the red glow of the angel with her still. It was intoxicating, like jasmine on a warm, summer evening, heady and exotic and she allowed herself some time to just be. Finally her mind focused on what the crimson being had said. She remembered the angel calling them all by name and stating that, although they were very much in this together, they each had a specific part to play. Rosie had found this to be a validating experience. If she was honest, up to now - in spite of everything - she had still felt as though Xander was the 'A-Lister' and she and Dan were supporting actors in whatever it was they seemed to be caught up in. This angel had been clear that the three of them created a harmony as they all had different gifts to bring, and as such they would receive different revelations of truth.

Rosie remembered that Adon Olam had proclaimed her gift was of the heart. She knew this was true because it sat comfortably with her, her spirit agreed with it somehow. The Spirit of Truth had taken this to the next level, stating that Rosie was going to meet two other spirits as part of her preparation. They were female spirits and were called Counsel and Understanding. She would recognise them by their colours of green and yellow respectively. Dan was to be trained up by Might and Fear, who were both masculine spirits and were the colours of blue and violet. These spirits complemented his calling of faith and would complete his strand of the three chord rope Adon Olam had spoken of. Xander's calling was one of vision and the spirits that were to come to him were Wisdom, a female spirit coloured orange, and the masculine spirit of Knowledge who was indigo. It was as if Xander linked the gentleness of Rosie and the boldness of Dan, completing the circle. When they had been back to Olam for this purpose, the Spirit of Truth would return to them again and . . .

Rosie's heart seemed to skip a beat. And what? What would come next? She hardly dared think about it as this part of their future plan had not been divulged.

"One step at a time, Rosie," she cautioned herself, as she reached for her phone to call Xander and Dan to share what the spirit had told her.

Chapter 34: Option Two

Yesterday Xander had had a fascinating chat with Rosie. It was good to hear her so enthused and excited. He was similarly motivated by her disclosure about the two spirits he was to meet. He had tried, and failed, to enter Olam in his dreams last night and woke early feeling restless. He wanted to get on with his training, but one thing he was beginning to realise was, you could not rush this place or force your way in through any effort on your own part. There appeared to be a timing and a pace that were not to be interfered with. Engaged with, yes, but not dictated to.

Unable to stand the prospect of looking at his ceiling, and the fine cobweb that stretched from the top of his lampshade to he couldn't quite make out where, Xander got up and went downstairs. It was 6.30, not a time he was used to seeing - particularly since finishing his exams and embarking on a seemingly endless summer that wasn't a summer!

"Dad! You startled me!" Xander jumped as he walked in to the kitchen to see his father sat at the oak table where they ate their meals together - or used to, back when home was a happier place. "I didn't hear you get up."

Xander's father stirred and looked up.

"What time is it?" he asked, barely registering his son. His eyes were circled with shadow and so was his chin. Had he been there all night, Xander wondered?

"It's 6.30, Dad. Are you ok? You look like you haven't slept."

Finally something changed in his father's face and he went back in to parent mode and smiled.

"Oh, not long. I mean, I got up a little while ago." He tried to look breezy and carefree and Xander both loved and hated him for it. Loved his father for trying to protect him from his own failures and disappointments and hated him at the same time for lying to him and treating him like a kid. "Do you want some pancakes?"

"Sure. Let's do it together."

They took their breakfast in to the sitting room and put on the news.

"After the break," stated a chirpy young woman in a floral fitted dress, with glossy, bouncy chestnut hair, "we will be talking to the Prime Minister and the founder of the Collective, Scarlett Tang. See you in a few moments." Xander sat forward in his seat.

"Scarlett?" he said, reflexively, then noticed his dad was looking searchingly at him. "Oh, I heard she'd left the Collective," he added, hurriedly, sitting back and trying to look nonchalant.

"What do you know about all this, son?" He had not fooled his father, he could see. This was the first time in almost two years that he was facing the reality that he would either have to tell a bare-faced lie or come clean. His heart was pounding and he knew that his expression had already betrayed him. He had no choice but to plump for good old option two.

"Well . . " he began, thinking quickly on his feet to find a way of telling the truth without going in to too much detail. "She came in to school, as I think you know. I did meet her and I did go along to some of the meetings, but it was no big deal. She left the organisation a couple of months ago for personal reasons and after my exams I wasn't at school or hanging out with the same people, so I stopped going."

There was a weighty silence in which Xander was willing his father to leave it there and not to ask any more questions. Unfortunately that was not going to happen, he realised, his heart sinking, as his dad asked, "Just how involved were you in all of this? Does your mother know? It's not dodgy is it?" He looked mistrustful, concerned. There was a hint of something else as well; guilt, Xander recognised sadly, suddenly understanding that his father was feeling contrite for being so wrapped up in his own problems that he hadn't noticed his only child being sucked in to some kind of cult.

He immediately tried to lighten the mood and reassure his father, "No Dad, no. Honestly, it was harmless. We would get together and share our dreams for things, our hopes, you know. It was quite utopian really. It was good to have a positive place to be . . . . till it all went . . . . well, till Scarlett left. She was special, Dad. She helped me to believe in things." He smiled at his dad, thinking about the irony of their role reversal - now he was being the protective one!

Breathing deeply, Xander's dad looked searchingly at his son, trying to gauge the level of bull being heaped upon him before turning back to the television. "Well, let's just see what they have to say then, shall we?"

Chapter 35: Breaking News

"Welcome back," smiled the overly exuberant, perky brunette. "We are honoured to be joined this morning by Peter Nixon, our Prime Minister," she spoke as if she were introducing Hollywood royalty, "and Scarlett Tang. Many of you will have heard of the Collective - particularly those of you with teenage children - she was its founder and she has kindly agreed to be here this morning to discuss a new programme to be rolled out across the country in September. Good morning Prime Minister, Ms Tang. What can you tell us about your exciting plans for the new academic year?"

Smiling his Galaxy-smooth grin, Nixon looked straight at the camera. "Thank you Monica, good morning. We are building on the good work started by Scarlett over the last two years. Would you like to begin Scarlett?"

Xander looked intently at her. He knew in his heart that it couldn't possibly **be** her, but the likeness and mannerisms were uncanny. It was a dangerous weapon that Nixon possessed in this Shapeshifter character.

"Thank you Peter," she looked coyly at the camera. "We began the Collective as a means to tackle the problems faced by young people. We wanted them to have something to believe in, something to own.

Initially the project relied on relaxation methods and some children found this difficult to access, so we have come together," she nodded towards Peter who bowed his head slightly, "to offer children the opportunity to get involved right from their own schools. The benefits of the Collective without the need for mastering meditative techniques."

"So where do you come in, Prime Minister?" asked the young anchor, careful to show her best side to camera whilst apparently flirting with the handsome and charming - and famously single - Mr. Nixon.

"Well, Monica," that smile again, "as you know, it is no secret that I have been involved in the Collective almost from its inception. I was stirred by Scarlett's vision and keen to use my powers as Education Minister to put the organisation on the map. Education is still very close to my heart, as is the plight of the young," he seemed to be flirting back and this did not go unnoticed by the young anchor. "I have made it my mission to ensure that this generation of young people will not have to grow up facing the same problems and uncertainties as their parents. Having something to believe in is Scarlett's special gift to these young people and we want to capitalise on that and take it a step further; make them masters of their own destinies by enrolling them in the organisation so they are forever connected and continually inspired. All secondary schools will now have the Collective as part of the curriculum. By that,

I mean that we will be encouraging them to adopt the methods of positive thinking and meditation that Scarlett has become synonymous with. There will be a room in each school that will be there for the facilitation of more strategic and specific visualisations."

"Sorry, can I interrupt you there, Prime Minister. There will be some people unfamiliar with the terminology you are using. Could you clarify what you mean by visualisations, please?"

"Of course," he responded, looking mildly irritated by the intrusion in to his carefully manicured speech. "Historically, children would meditate together and visualise the thing that they wanted to see achieved. What we want to do now is create an atmosphere within schools where children are encouraged to operate on that positive level as a matter of course, but, when more specific needs arise, they can access a designated room where a guide will be available at all times to help them engage with that vision and boost it through to fulfilment. The guides are available to all children, not just - as in the previous incarnation of the Collective - those children who were able to access, thorough meditation, a higher spiritual plane. We feel this is a much more inclusive and altogether positive step."

"And are the guides you speak about teachers, Prime Minister? What sort of training have they had?

Presumably they will need to deal with all manner of social and emotional issues?"

Xander looked intently at Nixon, but his face remained friendly and relaxed, giving nothing away.

"I can assure you, Monica, I have personally overseen the training of those concerned. It is my deepest desire that our children are kept safe and well in the school environment, and the Collective is going a step further than anything that has ever been seen in schools in the past, in order to achieve that goal."

"Liar!" Xander thought, but he was careful not to give away anything else to his father.

"Oh, I hope you didn't take any offence, Prime Minister," Monica looked at him anxiously. "Nobody could possibly doubt the altruistic motives you have where this nation and its children are concerned. We are forever in your debt."

"How kind of you to say, Monica. No offence taken, and I want no thanks for doing my job. It is an honour to serve my country." He bowed a sickening bow and Xander could watch no more.

"I like him," his father declared. "Where are you going, son?"

Chapter 36: Venting

"Did you see the news?"

"Yes. I can't believe he's wheeled out Shapeshifter for Scarlett again, and so publically! There must be a law against that!"

He's probably found a way round that, Rosie, he leaves nothing to chance. But that's not what I meant. At least we know his game plan now. He's going to be using his guides in this realm, in the schools. He must have hundreds of them. How are we going to fight that? There's three of us!" Xander felt overwhelmed by the prospect of what lay ahead. The enormity of it was just now dawning on him, along with a hefty dose of anger that this man in the public eye, this elected and respected man, had the whole nation eating out of his hand - even his own parents!

"We don't have to fight it here, Xander," Rosie stated, with a wisdom which extended far beyond her understanding. Her encounter with the Spirit of Truth had released something within her, opened up a neural pathway which had previously been disconnected. "We would not have been recruited if it was hopeless. We have no idea what support and power is at our disposal. Let's just wait and see before we write anything off as impossible."

"**Can** we do this Rosie?" Xander asked, almost ashamed of himself for saying it but feeling secure enough in his friendship with her to put it out there. There was a long pause and he felt as though even his heart was poised, missing a beat as it hovered in suspended animation, waiting for her to respond. "Rosie?"

"I heard you," came the reply. "You took me by surprise, that's all. You're the positive one, Xander. You're the one with the answers and the ideas. It's usually me asking the questions, the scared and insecure one."

"Sorry," he admitted, sheepishly.

"Don't be. It's ok. You know, for once I'm in a position to encourage you and build you up. To say, 'Yes, it's going to be ok.' We can do this Xander, because we're together. That's why we need each other because none of us has all the answers. We need unity; with each other, with the Brightness, with the Seven, it's the key to this. We have something that Peter Nixon does not and will never have. We have each other. His greatest strength - his independence - will become his greatest weakness. This generation doesn't just need a Prime Minister or a leader, it needs a father; someone to believe in it, love it and encourage it, not exploit it. Nixon doesn't know what that means and because of that very fact, he will fail."

Xander knew he had just witnessed something remarkable and potent. He had heard it, building and gaining a voice as Rosie spoke. It was the Truth.

Chapter 37: Wisdom and Knowledge

Xander lay on his bed. His parents had both gone out - Dad, somewhat reluctantly, to work and Mum to visit a friend. He had been stirred by Rosie's pep talk and it had replayed in his mind over and over. He was ready to go back to Olam, something had changed in him. He was ready, but a little anxious about what was to come. He breathed in deeply through his nose and crossed his feet - which were on the verge of hanging over the end of his bed. He had grown another centimetre or two over the Summer, during his temporary hibernation. He closed his eyes and tried to still his hectic thoughts, to round them up and chorale them in to various more manageable places. It was a soothing exercise and he felt himself start to relax. This in turn encouraged him to attempt to slacken every muscle from his head to his toes. His body was flooded with peace and he was just on the verge of dropping off when he felt himself transition in to Olam.

At least he assumed it was Olam. It was not familiar to him though, as he seemed to be in a garden. He had a vague memory of Scarlett talking about visiting a garden, so he went with it. It appeared to be evening time, as the plants and borders were flooded with a golden orange glow similar to early Autumn light. This light brought the colours to life and cast interesting shadows. There was a high flint wall running along to his left and in a recess in the wall a short distance away, he could see a bench. He felt drawn to it and walked slowly in its direction, marvelling at the fat buzz of bees and soft musical chorus of the birds that both sounded familiar and yet more melodious and varied than he had ever previously discerned. As he walked, he felt as though the flowers almost imperceptibly turned their heads in his direction, watching him; willing him to reach the bench. He stopped walking and an eerie silence seemed to descend upon the garden. He thought he must be imagining it or dreaming, for how could a garden respond to him in this way? It was as though his essence was essential to the life of the garden and as he started to move again, the hum and energy of the garden resumed. He was incredulous, it was more than his limited head-knowledge could understand or explain and he felt as if his jaw had physically dropped in response to this impossible phenomena.

"You came," a beautiful woman sat on his left and Xander jumped and stood up again with alarm, not realising until that moment that he had even sat down. She smiled warmly at him, her eyes deep pools of knowledge and in that moment Xander realised that she was the source of the golden light which illuminated this place.

"Who are you?" Xander stammered slightly, somewhat in awe of her. He sank back down on the bench as his legs seemed to have given up the desire to support him.

"I am known here as Wisdom. I will be one of your guides and preparers of the way."

"Is this your home? Am I still in Olam?"

"You are in Ma'on, the realm of ministering angels. But all realms here are symbiotic in their interconnection."

"How does this work?" Xander asked, uncertain. "Rosie said that we were to be visited by two Spirits each who would teach us, so that together we could defeat Nixon. I don't understand how all this is going to work."

"You worry too much, Xander. Do not focus on Nixon, he is a symptom of the current climate. Our battle is less tangible than the thing which you have perpetuated in your head. There is a time and a place for everything and for all things to work together. You are part of the fabric of something much more organic and harmonious than you are used to witnessing. You must trust us to help you."

At that precise moment, Xander became aware of a change in the light that surrounded him and he heard another, deeper voice to his right.

"You must listen to her voice, Xander. Wisdom is an invaluable friend. You must be able to perceive her resonance though, not just her words." He spun around on his seat to see another, taller, masculine figure who emanated the deepest purple hue that reminded Xander of taffeta and exotic birds' feathers.

"And who are you?" he asked, with more boldness than he felt.

"I am Knowledge. We are partners. You cannot truly have one without the other." Knowledge smiled at him and from the way he spoke, Xander felt that Wisdom was the one in charge!

"What are you going to do?" Xander was surprised that he didn't feel any fear or apprehension about being flanked by these beautiful and powerful looking beings.

"Complete your education, my boy!" Knowledge stated, winking playfully at Xander. "Are you ready?"

At that moment a butterfly fluttered around in front of Xander before landing on his hand. He looked down at it, its wings gently pulsating. There was no weight to it, it was only because he could see it that he knew it was there at all. He closed his eyes to see if he still knew that it was perched so delicately on his finger and with a whoosh he was drawn backwards, out of himself, out of time and in to an eternal place among the stars where things that he had never known became real to him and he understood deep and unsearchable truths. New neural pathways formed and a bond was created within him which linked him with universal Truth. He felt like Neo in 'The Matrix', as download after download created layer upon layer in his being, like a stratigraphic rock formation. He felt alive; he felt whole; he felt real. And in that place, he closed his eyes and drifted through galaxies and time to come home.

Back in his room, Xander allowed himself to slowly come round from his encounter. As he became more aware of his physically surroundings, his eyes were drawn to the window. He smiled as he saw a butterfly, dancing weightlessly like a papery talsiman, this side of the glass.

Chapter 38: A Worrying Development

"What is it that you want with me, Master? I have a lot to accomplish in a short time." Nixon barely disguised the impatience he felt at being summoned by the demon king.

Moloch sat on his throne, trying to ignore the tone he had detected, but a hot flash of anger crossed his face all the same.

"If I am keeping you from something, then please, be my guest." Sarcasm dripped off his tongue like a bitter syrup. Silence followed as the two would-be masters decided upon the wisdom and value of a face-off.

Concluding that now was not the time to lose favour with Moloch, Nixon conceded. "Forgive me, Master. It has been a stressful time. There is a lot riding on this." This wasn't a sign of weakness, he told himself, merely a matter of timing. Shows of strength need not always be overt - and it had taken considerable strength to keep silent. "What would you like to share with me?"

It was not that Moloch trusted him any more for this show of obsequiousness, but he was accustomed to being the top dog and had a strong sense of his own importance. Nixon backing down was a boost to his vanity.

"I have been monitoring Ma'on, the realm of the angels."

"And?" Nixon fought to keep the irritation out of his voice. Was this really what he had been summoned here for? He wasn't interested in angels; in his opinion they were weak and sickening. He was only concerned with what he could use and manipulate.

"And . . . ." Moloch raised his voice like a teacher dealing with a rebellious and petulant child, "there is something going on. An unprecedented level of activity. They too are working with the children."

"But what can they possibly achieve? They are probably just answering some poor kid's prayer about their sick cat. What's got you so riled? They are nothing to us, we have the supremacy here."

"I'm telling you not to discount them, Peter. I'm also telling you that it would be in your best interests to find out who they are working with."

There was something in his tone and in his face that got Peter's attention. There was history there, he could see the ghost of it. As much as he didn't want to buy in to this melodramatic notion of Moloch's, something told him to take heed. And by children, he was pretty sure he knew who the demon was talking about.

Chapter 39: Tightening the Net

Peter Nixon had a deeply held belief in his own abilities and he did not consider he had taken any unnecessary or compromising risks where his plans were concerned. Still, it didn't hurt to cross a few tees. He had been sitting in his office for the last hour mulling over the conversation he was about to have with David Moorcroft, head of MI5 and Sir Anthony Dymock, Security Advisor to the Prime Minister. They were late.

The Prime Minister stared at the door with a growing sense of annoyance simmering beneath his carefully manicured persona. One thing he struggled to tolerate was poor time-keeping. He shifted his position in his chair, crossing and uncrossing his ankles where they rested, stretched out under the desk and bringing his fingers together in a steeple. Behind him - although they would not on this occasion be visible to anyone else in the room - were his now constant companions, Naamah and Shapeshifter. The latter bent down to whisper in to Nixon's right ear. A smile played gently at the corner of the world leader's mouth before twitching in to a grin. There was an ease between them that had become increasingly obvious as their bond had strengthened. The demonic forces Nixon partnered with had become a permanent extension of him and he respected their input.

"Let's just see if they are willing to support their Prime Minister first. I do not need unnecessary casualties at this time - although I value your commitment to the cause, and if I had my way . . . ."

The buzzer on his internal phone indicated that his guests had arrived. Rearranging his expression to eliminate all signs of his frustration, Nixon forced his mouth in to a smile and strode across the deep piled carpet of his office, yanking open the door which led through to the atrium where they would be exchanging pleasantries with Angela, his assistant slash Rottweiler - nobody got through her except through the proper channels and he valued her ability to take charge of even the most belligerent member of the House of Lords.

"David; Sir Anthony," he extended his hand generously. "Welcome. I do hope you have not been caught up in traffic?" The reference to their delay was thinly veiled and it did not go unnoticed.

"Apologies, Prime Minister, for our lateness," bowed Sir Anthony Dymock, glancing at his watch. "Completely unavoidable I can assure you. Blessed traffic! The congestion charge may need addressing!" The three men chuckled, knowing it was something they could all claim expenses for.

"The cameras have their uses though, gentlemen, which brings us nicely on to what I want to talk about." They had walked back in to Nixon's office and he gestured for them to sit in two leather Juliet armchairs facing his desk. "Would you like some refreshment?"

"No thank you," responded the Security Advisor, taking it upon himself to speak for both of them, to which Moorcroft looked a little crestfallen. "Let's proceed shall we?"

"Marvellous!" echoed Nixon, sitting down with measured purposefulness. "I wanted to talk to you about the extra surveillance cameras in situ across the nation. Are they all operational?"

"But Prime Minister," Dymock sat forward with a slight expression of alarm on his face, "I thought we agreed it would not be necessary to use them after all."

"My dear Sir Anthony," Nixon turned not just his face on the man, but the full extent of his charm as well. "These have been troubling times, need I not remind you. This country is sitting on a knife edge and although it may look as if things have settled down somewhat since those horrific events in the Commons, you cannot deny that we have a duty to protect this nation."

"But was it not just there as a precaution? Have we really reached the point where that kind of level of surveillance is absolutely imperative?" interjected the Head of M15, looking equally concerned.

"Would you rather wait for something else to happen, gentlemen? We cannot shut the stable door after the horse has bolted. David, you of all people know that. Besides, people want to be protected, they just don't necessarily want to know how." There was a pause, loaded with tension and no small amount of unspoken pressure from the Prime Minister. "I would like the extra cameras turned on and I would like daily reports concerning any person or persons perceived to be a threat to either national security or to this government." Another pause as Nixon allowed his wishes to sink in. "Are we all on the same page?"

"Yes Prime Minister," nodded the two senior advisors in unison. "Consider it done."

"I knew you were the right men for the job," smiled Nixon gracefully, standing to indicate that their meeting was over. "Now, if that is all, gentlemen, I have much to be getting on with; as have you. Good day." He shook their hands firmly then broke eye contact, maintaining his ground behind the desk before sitting down again and giving the papers in front of him his full attention as they shuffled uncertainly off.

Chapter 40: Further Security Measures

He felt happier knowing that the surveillance cameras would be maintaining a 24/7 in depth monitoring of anyone who may be perceived to be a challenge to his authority - that was something that M15 took very seriously and it comforted him to know that they had his back. He was not someone who generally succumbed to paranoia, but there was something about the way Moloch had behaved at their last meeting that made him feel that he needed to take his protection more seriously. He also knew enough about the spirit realms to know that it was not just in the natural realm that he needed to be vigilant; he was not naive enough to assume that this was all he needed to do. Nixon turned to face his most loyal subjects and to gain from them some insight in to what he may be up against.

"Moloch warned me that there may be a threat of a different kind to contend with. What can you tell me about it?"

This was a new experience for him, asking for help, and he felt a little uncomfortable needing to even propose the question. But there was no sense in being precious about it. If there were things you couldn't sort out for yourself, he realised, then he would be foolish to discount the possibility that there were others who may be able to widen his perspective or offer information about things he had never considered.

Shapeshifter looked puzzled for a second, then asked, "Are you referring to the Tang woman? I assure you, she is no longer a threat to us. I have been monitoring her closely and she has made no attempt to either engage with the Brightness or re-enter the realms of Olam or Ma'on."

Nixon decided to let the 'us' in Shapeshifter's little speech slide for now, although it stuck in his skin like a thorn. The audacity of him, to assume that their arrangement had anything to do with equality! It was like a Roman soldier regarding himself to be on a par with the Emperor!

Swallowing the gall that rose up within him, Nixon asked, "Has she had any visitors?"

"Only that boy. Why?"

Nixon immediately knew to whom Shapeshifter was referring and it took all of his self control not to grab the demon by its scrawny little neck. "Xander? He's still meddling is he? Why wasn't I told?" His eyes were black as a crow's and showed the same evil and murderous intent.

Suddenly Shapeshifter was not as cocky and self-assured as he had been. He felt the full intensity of the glare and was confused. Why was Master turning on him? He was a loyal subject? He was Nixon's greatest advocate, surely he knew that? His answer reflected his rapid and unforeseen loss of confidence. "I'm not sure, my Lord. But he has been to see her . . . so I am told." The conclusion to his sentence was added as an afterthought, to separate him from whatever wrath may be forthcoming.

Unexpectedly, Nixon did not erupt with vengeance on Shapeshifter, but turned his withering gaze on Naamah instead. "I want you to visit him as only you can, in a dream. Open him up. Be careful though, he must not suspect you."

"Master, it would be my honour. You can trust me with this, I assure you." Naamah bowed low, her golden hair brushing against Nixon's shoulder, and Shapeshifter seethed with jealous indignation.

"And find out who he's working with. I don't want any surprises. You have underestimated him by keeping his activities from me and I will not tolerate any more incompetence. What is the point of you," he spat out, scathingly, "if you fail to police the realms you inhabit? I will not have you here at the expense of compromising this project." He turned back to his desk as he said this and waved them both away with a dismissive flick of the wrist as he turned his attention back to the daily mound of papers which required his particular attention. If Shapeshifter and Naamah had felt they possessed any kind of favour or elevated position in the rankings of Nixon's following, they were left in no doubt now that such expectations had been vain and foolish.

Chapter 41: Dan

Of the three of them, Dan probably had the least experience of supernatural events, but he was not fazed by it. The next day they were due to meet at Xander's as arranged, and Dan was keen to have something to share with them of his own experiences in the realms they were discovering together. Rosie had phoned him and told him what the Spirit of Truth had shared with her about their particular teachers. Dan had been waiting ever since for a summons from Might or Fear. He was not sure what to expect, they sounded a bit intimidating to him and he was slightly concerned about what he would have to go through as part of his training. But Adon Olam had told him that his strength lay in his faith, so he tried to trust that whatever it was, and however it came, that he would be ready for it.

He must have been in quite a deep sleep because, in spite of the intensity of his dream, he did not wake. He found himself in a fishing boat on a stormy sea. There were men on the deck in deep yellow oilskins, slick with water, shouting in to the squally wind and battered by needles of icy rain. The sky and sea had made some kind of agreement whereby neither of them would divulge where one ended and the other began. The boat churned and rocked violently on the waves and Dan stood, fighting to maintain his balance. He was exposed to the rawness of everything the elements could chuck at him and felt it with every cell of his body, and yet the men working on the ship seemed to be oblivious to his existence. Realising that nobody had seemed to notice his presence there, Dan fought the rising fear that if no one could see him, then equally no one would discern the risk that he may be washed overboard by the swollen and vengeful sea.

"What are you afraid of?" It was the strangest thing; through the clamour and tumult of the storm, he could hear a clear and distinct voice which seemed to be speaking in to his very soul. He spun around in to the wind, feeling the sting of rain on his now streaming wet face. A being with a rich violet aura stood beside him, apparently unmoved by the squall.

Dan thought for a moment, fighting the urge to reply with the most instinctive or obvious response. Even in that moment, he knew he was being tested and snapping back with an acerbic retort would not be helpful.

"Of being invisible," he finally acknowledged, knowing that this was a deeply held observation which covered more than just this moment.

"I see you, Dan," the man stated, looking deep in to his eyes. It was an intensely profound and inspirational juncture, in which Dan suddenly felt himself engage with his potential as a young man; as if his DNA had reached out in to something in the universe and felt a reciprocal strand extend itself in his direction, whereby a satisfying 'click' attested to their union. A hollow place had been filled. The boy was instantly reassured and felt peace well up within him. The precariousness of his position seemed to hold no fear for him in that second where their eyes connected and Dan caught a glimpse of eternity. It was the opposite of what he had expected to happen. He assumed, as he heard the Spirit's words, that they would bring a sense of external reassurance which only comforted him on the level of circumstance; but all that ameliorated him now, came from within.

"Why am I here?" Dan asked, almost unaware now of the nightmarish scenario he was a part of.

"Because we have a mandate to train you to become sons."

"Sons of what?"

"Sons of Destiny; sons of Truth. The Spirit of Truth has overall authority and is the key to your success. But to be fully able to express your identity, you must be trained by the Seven Spirits. Time is short, therefore we have assigned to you two spiritual fathers - Fear and Might. You must face your fear Dan, in order to engage with your inner strength. You will not just liberate yourself in the process, but your generation as well. Might will meet you at the moment in which your fears are taken captive."

"What do you mean?" Dan asked, feeling a little alarmed as he was starting to realise why he was here. Since he was small, he had had a fear of drowning after an incident at the seaside on a family holiday, where the inflatable dingy he had been playing in was caught simultaneously by a freak wave and a strong gust of wind, causing it to flip over and throw him into the water, trapping him underneath. He had struggled to find his way back to the surface and then out from under the boat before being rescued by a nearby swimmer - as neither of his parents had seen what had occurred.

The Spirit of Fear looked deep in to his soul, before speaking. "You are not alone, Dan," he said as a huge wave crashed over the trawler and washed him overboard in to the boiling sea. Dan did not even have time to take a breath before he was plunged in to the icy water. His body screamed at him to perform the instinctive physiological action of breathing, exacerbated by the shock of the circumstances and the cold water, but he fought it desperately, trying to let his brain evaluate which way was up without overriding or confusing it with waves of panic. The seconds seemed to be ticking audibly and leisurely by in the eerie, muffled sounds of the underwater world, so sharply contrasting with the barrage of noise created by the storm.

"Think!" he commanded himself. Instinctively he knew he must take his fear of death captive and he summoned all of his concentration and determination to picture the fear as a prisoner of war; manacled and rendered impotent. As he did so, he felt something under him, pushing him upwards. He panicked initially, kicking out as he looked down in to the darkness. A bluish face stared up at him, speaking in to his subconscious.

"I am the Spirit of Might, Dan. Do not fight me, use me."

Dan knew this was a strategic statement and he drew all his energy deep in to himself, felt the force beneath him, and somehow fused himself with it to propel him up towards the surface. His face broke through the waves and he gulped and gasped, hungrily drawing air in to his aching, burning lungs.

Suddenly he was back in his room with a faint blue and violet light accompanying him.

"What have you learnt?" asked the otherwise silent room.

"Not to let my fears rule or define me, but to channel them and overcome them with the might of my faith and belief in who I am."

"You are correct. You are not alone, Dan, for we are one." With that, the glow was extinguished and he sat there, on his bed, panting and shivering from the shock of his encounter and the intensity of his experience. Dan knew with complete certainty, that something within himself had just been rewritten.

Chapter 42: The Dream

Whilst Dan had been having his encounter with his destiny, Xander had been experiencing a dream of an entirely different kind. He was back in the garden again. It was beautiful and fragrant and busy with life; he could taste the green, like a newly clipped hedge, but there was something about it which didn't quite feel right to him - like a piece of music ever so slightly off key. He couldn't put his finger on it, but he found himself - in the dream - examining his surroundings with a more critical eye, looking for familiarity or a point of reference. So absorbed was he that he was startled by a voice at his side, not having been aware of anyone approaching.

"Welcome Xander."

"Where am I?" he asked, feeling guarded.

"Where do you think you are, Xander? Among friends. I am your encourager. Come; let's walk."

There was something about her beguiling beauty and honey-dipped voice that was familiar to him. It was precisely the sense that he had some kind of conversancy with this being and this place that was willing him to let his guard down. But he still could not decide whether or not it felt right. What was it?

In spite of his reservations, he fell in to step with the woman. He found her to be enchanting and convivial and he felt himself starting to relax. His focus - which had been completely and earnestly fixed on finding some flaw with this place - was now one hundred per cent centred upon her. He glanced sideways at her, shyly, not even believing her capable of being anything other than she appeared and asked, "Are you one of the Seven?"

There it was! For the briefest second it was as if a cloud passed across her countenance and the light went out in her eyes. Xander almost missed it, she had recovered herself so quickly, but it was in that instant that her tell was revealed and he knew exactly where he had seen her before: in the Castle. She was one of Nixon's guides.

"Tell me, Xander," she asked him sweetly, salvaging her serenity, "who have you met already?"

This was some kind of fact finding mission of Nixon's; of that, Xander was absolutely sure. They were no longer under the radar and the knowledge of that sent his heart beating faster so he could hear the blood pumping in his ears. Fighting to obscure any evidence of his inner turmoil from his face, he tried to think quickly about what he should do. His mind whirred to process the options which lay before him. Option one: say nothing and play dumb; option two: tell them everything in the hope of unsettling them;

option three: play along adding a heavy dose of misinformation. Xander quickly discarded option one - it would achieve nothing and instantly alert Naamah to the fact that he had recognised her. Option two felt like something he wanted to do in the impulse of the moment, in order to shake Nixon's vain certainty in his unspeakable scheme - but showing their hand would ultimately not be a wise move. Wise. Here was his chance to utilise the training he had received from the Spirit of Wisdom. But it was not like school. He had not been physically taught how to respond and given the tools to perform his task. Somehow, though, he knew the answer inhabited him; he just had to lay hold of it. That all he would ever need to know or do was already inside him.

"I have met with the Spirit of Truth," he replied, deciding to start with something plausible. "They told me that I was going to meet other spirits here who would reveal things for the coming days."

"And who have you met so far?"

"You are the first. Did you say you were the Spirit of Encouragement? I wasn't told who would come, just to expect them one by one."

"Yes," Naamah responded, barely disguising her glee, "I am one of the Seven. What are you expecting to learn?"

"Well, how to reach the Brightness. That's what I'm here for. It seems more difficult now than it was in the Castle. I just want to go back to how things were."

"Of course you do. What about your friends?"

"My friends?" Xander looked at her innocently.

"Do they come with you?" Naamah's expression was gentle and kind, but Xander could feel a dark force operating unseen, trying to draw information from him. He resisted it.

"I honestly don't know what they are up to. I've kept myself to myself over the summer. It was difficult, you know, losing Scarlett and the Castle."

"Yes, yes, it must have been. We all felt the loss of it," Naamah added, quickly, trying to maintain the pretence.

"What have you come to teach me?" He looked directly at her, hoping his expression didn't call her out.

"I am here to encourage you to return to this location as often as you can. This garden is a healing place, it will help you to find what you seek." He searched her expression for any sense that she did not believe his cover. He couldn't read her at all. She bowed her head, keeping her eyes locked on to his and he bowed in return. He hated her more than ever;

hated her lies, her deception, her association with that man. He knew she was not one of the Seven and that she hadn't even used one of their names, but he didn't know what her intentions were. Was she trying to mislead him? Trap him? He looked around him and suddenly remembered what it was that felt wrong about this place - it was the light; it had no life as the Brightness did. He was suddenly alarmed by the knowledge that it was not just Naamah that was wrong about this dream, it was the whole setting he was in. He wanted to go now, before things got ugly - or she rumbled him.

Thinking quickly, Xander smiled and asked, "May I look round by myself? I just love walking in this garden and looking at the life here."

"Of course," she bowed again. "I look forward to meeting with you again here soon, to continue your education. We have so much to discuss." Then she was gone.

Xander did not hang around in that place. Fortunately he found it easy to return to the familiarity and safety of his room. His stomach felt as though it contained shards of cold glass. Things were escalating, of that he had no doubt. Now that they knew about the visits to the other realms, he felt sure they would be more closely monitored. This was not good news.

Chapter 43: Feedback

"Greetings, my Lord Overseer. I come with troubling news."

Adon Olam bowed graciously to both acknowledge and welcome the Spirit of Truth. He/she was tall and strong, yet feminine and gentle at the same time, like a Gothic cathedral. There was a continuous oscillation - like the soft undulating fronds of a deep sea coral - between male and female, sweeping majestically across the face and this proved to be both captivating and reassuring.

"It's about the boy. He has been visited this evening by one from the darkness."

"He is strong, do not worry. It was inevitable."

"Naamah is a master of deception, my Lord," the spirit stated with concern.

"He has received his preparation, we must have faith in him. You know as well as anyone that it is not in our power to prevent such interventions from occurring. Our role is to equip and support them. We cannot do it all for them, you know that. How they handle the challenges is at least as important as how they conduct themselves. Without adversity, how do we really know what we have learnt?"

"I do know that Master, of course. But we are so close now, I can feel it, yet our position is so precarious. What if they aren't ready?"

Adon Olam looked at the Spirit of Truth for a long time before he spoke. "We have known this time would come. We have tasted victory over the years and we have also known defeat. This is a battle we **cannot** lose and we must trust that the Brightness has made the right selections." His expression was grave and the Spirit of Truth could detect that even the Overseer himself did not have all the answers in these final days.

* * * * *

"Well? How did it go?" asked an impatient Nixon.

"It was puzzling, Master."

"Puzzling? Are you serious? I need more than that!" The Prime Minister's voice rose menacingly as he spoke.

"I'm sorry, my Lord. I could not read him; I could not tell. There was some kind of barrier there which I have not come across before. Usually I can read people like a book . . . ."

Nixon interrupted her sharply, "I don't care what you can **usually** do! That's of no use to me **now**!" The anger was rising, this was not what he wanted to hear.

"Either he knows nothing and he is merely there on some kind of nostalgic quest to rediscover his experiences with the Brightness, or . . . ."

"Or what?" The anger had given way to something else, uncertainty or concern, Nixon couldn't tell which but he was unable to keep it out of his voice.

"Or he is a consummate performer and he was playing me. If I had to guess, I'd say that boy knows more than he's letting on. He knew of the Seven, that in itself is alarming - although he didn't seem to know anything about them. I made up a name and I saw nothing in him to suggest he was suspicious."

"But you've already admitted you couldn't read him. Do you think they are working with him? The Seven?"

"It's possible, Master, yes. We may well have stirred up the realms to defend themselves. Historically, they have always partnered with man at such times."

Nixon looked concerned. "What kind of threat are they? Don't placate me with your vile deceptions, I want the truth!"

"I cannot say, my Lord. None of us have ever witnessed anything on this scale before. There are legends of a flood that will emancipate the Earth, but it has been spoken of for centuries and nothing has come of it. It is a story designed to cast fear in to our hearts and keep us from fully realising our own destiny. " Naamah tried to speak with conviction, but her encounter with Xander had unsettled her. There was something different about him, he had something which seemed to make him impervious to her charms and she was not accustomed to it.

Nixon sighed heavily and looked at his servant again with fresh eyes. Were they up to this after all, these creatures he had trusted to help him fulfil his plan? Would they fail him with their lies and their innate weakness? He had hoped for reassurance from Naamah's report, but all it had done was to make him doubt their competence. He hated having to rely upon anyone or anything. What else hadn't they told him about or prepared him for in their blind pursuit of power?

Naamah felt his hostility and his disgust and it pierced her black heart. "I am sorry I have failed you, Master." She looked down, ashamed.

Nixon was not feeble enough to fall for shows of emotional weakness, but he was forced to admit that a sense of unease had entered in to that place where most people have a heart. For the first time he wondered if he had an adversary who could challenge him. But a boy?

Chapter 44: Equipped

Rosie had enjoyed the brief respite at her Gran's house - she would have to go home though, after her planned meeting with Xander and Dan. She had not heard how things had gone with them and she had to admit that she was disappointed not to have had any follow up encounters from the spirit realm herself.

She looked across at the Mickey Mouse alarm clock on the dresser. He cheerfully pointed out that it was only six-thirty. It was a fresh morning with a slightly Autumnal feel and Rosie pulled up her knees and hugged them through the duvet. She heard her Gran stir and get up in the room next door, but she selfishly did not want to be with anyone right now.

In spite of not really having anything else to think about, Rosie was surprised how difficult it was to focus her thoughts specifically on Olam, where she was itching to go and complete her training. Her mind kept wandering off to puerile things, which frustratingly didn't really hold any interest for her.

"Focus!" she chastised herself, quietly. She looked round guiltily as she realised she had spoken out loud. Mickey didn't seem to care; he still grinned inanely at her, pointing his oversized fingers.

She took a deep breath and laid back against the pillows, trying to imagine herself back in Olam on one of its many paths. She closed her eyes and opened them again moments later to find herself in a room not unlike the Throne Room of the Castle. She blinked, thinking her eyes must still be closed and she was imagining it; but they weren't, whatever this place was she was really here. A strange being sat at the table in the middle of the room. It felt a bit like a war room, although she had no idea why that even occurred to her, she just seemed to know it.

"Welcome," said the being, who nodded slightly as she spoke. "I am Counsel."

Rosie felt like she was staring, but she couldn't help it. The spirit had three pairs of eyes on her head, spaced out on the horizontal plane, yet still managed to look serene and beguiling in the emerald light which emanated from her.

"You are wondering about the eyes, Rosie, aren't you?" she questioned. "Shall we get that bit out of the way?"

Rosie nodded mechanically, still captivated by her and unable to break her gaze.

"You need to be able to look upon any situation, Rosie, and decide if the counsel you offer is advice, knowledge or instruction. They are three different levels of expectation, requiring three different viewpoints. What you are being charged with requires a great level of discernment. Humans, generally speaking, have lost the ability to ascertain which counsel to offer when, but you will be given a special gift to implement this. Listen to your heart so you may know what to apply." The spirit leaned forward and touched Rosie's heart three times. She looked down, sensing a quickening and noticed that the flame which she had forgotten was there, now burned with a greenish tinge. When she looked up again, the beautiful being was gone.

Rosie stayed where she was, trying to take in what had just happened to her. She was gradually aware of what felt like rain on her face. She looked up but could see nothing out of the ordinary. The only perceivable difference was that the light in the room had changed from a natural light to a yellow glow and looking down at her skin, Rosie could see that it was gradually being covered with tiny, glistening fragments of gold. She rubbed her forearm and the gold seemed to be absorbed in to the surface of her skin. A resplendent figure materialised in the shimmering rain. She felt markedly different from anyone else Rosie had encountered so far, as she had this inexplicable ability of being able to appear as illusory and tangible simultaneously.

"I am Understanding," she said in a voice which seemed to be reverberating all around Rosie on a boundless wave of sound. "Absorb me in to every cell and fibre of your being." It was the most incredible experience Rosie had ever had, both intimate and fulfilling. She felt herself come alive on a Quantum level as she was showered in the golden mist. She first became aware of the cellular level of her body and this expanded to include the atoms with their electrons, protons and neutrons. She couldn't explain it, she just felt herself being awakened and taken further and further in to the sub-atomic structure of herself until she could literally feel the strings vibrating on the frequency of this incredible being before her within each quark. For the first time in her life she felt both completely herself and fully at one with all of creation. It was both liberating and empowering in a single moment. She laughed and felt her joy for this experience increase and overwhelm her. Just as it rose to an almost unbearable crescendo of intensity and she thought the hugeness of the realisation that the very fabric of the universe was not just made of the same things as her, but actually inhabited her somehow and she might burst from the revelation of it, she was back in the bedroom at her Gran's.

Rosie jumped off the bed as though she had been burned, exhaling loudly. She spun around, trying to get her bearings then glanced down at her right arm. It looked as if she had applied a shimmer tan to her skin. It glowed with life and light and she ran to the mirror to look at her face. Everything about her countenance shone and sang of the life she contained.

"Wow!" was all she could think to say.

Chapter 45: Saturday

"You're looking well, Darling. You must have had a good night!" Gran smiled warmly at Rosie as she sat down for breakfast.

"I am, thank you. Never felt better!" she smiled back. "Thanks for giving me this time. It's been really . . . . special."

"I love having you here, you know that. It's certainly been quiet around here since Grandad . . . ." The sentence remained unfinished, but they both knew how it ended. "You'll have to do it again. Soon." Gran squeezed her arm lovingly.

"I'd like that."

They sat and chatted together for a while about family, GCSE results - due next week - friends and sixth form until it was time for Rosie to head for the tube station and her meeting with the boys.

It was another miserable day. The kind of dampness that gets in to your bones. The trees had already given up any hope of Summer and their leaves were that sludgy, dirty green, as they hung off the branches like neglected washing. Even so, Rosie was still too excited by her visitation to allow it to affect her. People around her walked with their heads down and their hands thrust in to coat pockets, looking as grim as the weather. She wanted to run down the street and shout, "Don't be beaten. You are not forsaken! A new day is coming!" She restrained herself regrettably, wondering if she should not have just given vent to her emotions. But a voice in her heart confirmed her words and assured her that she was right to resist all at the same time; 'The day will come!'

* * * * *

It was so special to be able to sit together and share their experiences, buoyed up by the same excitement which had motivated their dreams in the Castle. It was the same and yet it was different. Then it had been like playing a game for which you only understood some of the rules: it was fun, but you didn't completely get it. Now it was more serious. They understood the rules, but they had realised that actually, this was not a game that they were playing.

"I thought it would be harder, somehow," Dan proclaimed. "Is that it do you think? Our training, I mean, is it complete?"

"I think it is, but I agree. I assumed training would require some kind of effort on our part, but it seems to be more about engaging with something that is already inside us." Xander looked at his friends for affirmation.

"I can't tell you how special it has been," Rosie added, her eyes shining with the joy she felt. "It's as if I finally know who I am. I thought the training was going to teach me to be something else, someone else; but it turns out everything is already there I just needed to unlock it."

Finally they sat in silence, exhausted from sharing and talking and wondering. After partaking in such remarkable encounters, it did not feel right to Xander to talk about his visit from Naamah. Rightly or wrongly, being an only child, Xander was used to dealing with things himself. Naamah had given him no reason to be concerned about the wellbeing of his friends, and even if they were on her radar, he felt he had deflected her interest away from them. No, if she was coming back, it would be for him and if that happened he would deal with it. He felt a brotherly protection for Rosie and did not want to squash her new found enthusiasm and confidence. There was a fragility about her that was part of what made her beautiful. As for Dan, he did not feel he had a deep enough personal relationship with him to share on this level. So he held his tongue, instead choosing to ask no one in particular, "What do we do now?"

Rosie immediately felt a responsibility to engage with this inquiry. Advice, knowledge or instruction? She closed her eyes and focused on the cellular level of her body. "Now we wait for the Spirit of Truth to draw us all together." Apparently, it was a question which required knowledge!

Chapter 46: Tzadok

Order exists in the most unexpected places and there was an order in the spirit realms which the young people had been visiting. The High Priest was Tzadok and he had governed this place since the beginning of time. He was aware that there were threats to his authority, sadly that is always true, it seems. Even the purest and most benevolent force has a challenger - just as the Brightness had. But there was a unifying thread in these realms which joined the forces of light together and bonded them in love. They had a selfless affection for one another and a deep and abiding love for mankind, as well as the desire to see them free from the destructive forces of Moloch and the like.

The High Priest's authority had been lost centuries ago in one of the realms, Machon. In spite of the benevolence of the others, this realm had the power to infect and disease everything else and it was this realm which they ultimately sought to contain and extinguish. Containment had been their only option up until now, but there was an unspoken agreement that as long as people chose to partner with the destructive forces of Machon, it would be allowed to exist - providing it did not interfere with the other levels. But something had shifted and Tzadok had seen it. There was a subtle deception in play which had begun with the crossing over of Moloch's guides in to the Castle. This breach was strictly against generations of protocol, but it highlighted an evolution in the wickedness of the world. It was no longer content to remain within the boundaries of universal acceptability; it was seeking domination. Tzadok could not let that happen; yet, as he roamed around over the Earth, he had been alarmed by how few people had engaged with the Truth. Was it apathy? Had they been anaesthetised by generations of mediocrity and low level disappointment or lack of expectation? Had they forgotten how to hope? Forgotten the Truth and relegated it to a legendary status? He felt ashamed that it had come to this. Had he failed? Had he been arrogant? Or too trusting? Yet he knew in his heart that people **had** to be free to choose.

"My Lord High Priest," it was Ethan, bowing low, who brought Tzadok out of his reverie.

"What news, Ethan?" he inquired, almost breathless with anticipation.

"Their education is complete, my Lord, and they are not alone. The nations have given up their fire carriers and many of them are children."

"Are we ready?"

"Not yet, my Lord Tzadok. But the countdown has begun."

Tzadok looked down through the rainbow coloured layers at the focal point of this whole conflict; a small blue and green ball spinning silently and majestically in space. He nodded approvingly.

Chapter 47: Results Day

Having agreed to keep themselves open to any advances from the Spirit of Truth, the children decided that the next thing they could do of any real value would be to use the time they went in to school to collect their GCSE results as an opportunity to have a bit of a scout around, to see what changes had been implemented by Nixon in their respective schools for the new term.

They had been told to come in to school at ten o'clock for their results and all three were excited - and a little apprehensive - to see what the culmination of two years of hard work had achieved. Xander had pretty much talked himself in to believing his would be down on the predictions due to the nature of what had been going on at the Castle during the exam period. Rosie, as usual, was more optimistic.

"You'll be fine," she reassured him, as he voiced this concern. "All things work together for good. You put the work in, so don't doubt yourself." He looked at her fondly as they stood in the line to register their names and collect their long-awaited results. Once again he was surprised by the level of wisdom and maturity this girl possessed. He made a mental note to stop being surprised by her, something had shifted in her; she had a boldness and confidence now. It wasn't arrogance, there was nothing repellent about it at all, it was humbling actually. He smiled.

"I thought I was the one who met Wisdom," he quipped. "Have you been meeting her secretly behind my back?"

Rosie laughed and punched him playfully in the arm, knowing that in boy talk, that was what constituted a compliment!

"Shall we sneak off now, whilst it's busy, and see what we can find?" Xander asked, the tone of his voice becoming more serious and furtive. His face registered it too, as he glanced around conspiratorially. "We can come back later, when it's quieter, to get our results."

"Yeah, good idea," Rosie whispered back. "I don't think anyone will notice us slip out."

They left the queue in the sports hall separately, so as to minimize the risk of being observed, and met at reception. They had no idea where the Collective would be located, but Xander guessed that they may use the same room that he and Rosie had been meeting in for months to access the Castle on behalf of the school. Their Head teacher, Mr Mason, had been very supportive and, having met Scarlett in person, he was keen to facilitate things for them. It seemed as good a place as any to begin their search.

He was right. Outside the room was a newly attached plaque, reading 'The Collective'. Gingerly, Xander opened the door and peered in. It was dark inside due to the fact that the room had no windows to allow in natural light. He had never thought about it before, but under its new guise it made the room feel claustrophobic and unsettling. He reached for the switch and was relieved when the fluorescent light burst in to life and washed the room with its sterile glow. The room was void of furniture except for a filing cabinet in the corner.

"Shall we open it?" he asked, uncertainly.

"We have to," Rosie replied, not giving away any misgivings she may feel about breaking and entering.

Xander walked over and pulled at the top drawer; it was locked. "Damn it!" he exclaimed. "What now?"

Without hesitating, Rosie pulled a hairpin out of her bun and strode over to Xander, purposefully elbowing him aside.

"Make way for the professionals!" she exclaimed, a recalcitrant expression playing across her mouth which surprised and delighted Xander.

"You're kidding, right?" he laughed. "You, Miss Butter-wouldn't-melt, can pick a lock?"

"How hard can it be?" she replied, not looking up as she concentrated on the job in hand.

As it turned out, harder than it looked. In spite of their best efforts, neither of them could get in to the cabinet. Xander bashed the top drawer with the flat of his palm out of frustration. It was then that he noticed a tiny corner of paper just poking out of the drawer. He pulled at it with his finger tips, but his hands were too big and clumsy and his nails too short.

"Can you get this?" he asked Rosie, standing aside. She picked at it and managed to get it about a quarter of the way out on the diagonal before it got jammed in the lock mechanism. It appeared to be some kind of contract.

"What is it?" she asked Xander, concerned by the implications.

"I think Nixon is planning on getting some kind of legal consent for whatever it is he's doing. Isn't that just like him? That changes things! We need to speak to Dan, see if he's found out any more at his school. Come on, we can't stay here and risk being seen."

Carefully he pushed the paper back in and they left the room, switching off the light and shutting the door, but forgetting the hairpin that lay bent out of shape on top of the cabinet.

Chapter 48: Answers

It should have been a time for celebration. They had all texted their parents their respective exam results - happily the three of them had passed everything, though A's were in short supply. Rosie was most pleased with her B in Maths, which she attributed to the Brightness and a download that had occurred during her very first encounter with it. Now they were sat in the Coffee House, near Dan's school, discussing the next course of action.

"Did you find anything at your school?" Rosie asked, after explaining what they had seen.

"It sounds much the same as your experience," he said. A locked filing cabinet - sadly my hairdo does not require lock picking paraphernalia!" he quipped, running his hands through his product-enhanced, carefully arranged hair.

"Why a contract though?" Rosie was still puzzled by it. "Xander thinks it's a legal thing."

"I agree with you on this one. Nixon wants to cover himself and if the beast Scarlett said she saw in the Castle has anything to do with this, then I would guess it requires something in return for empowering Nixon. Maybe a contract will satisfy it, like a sacrifice or something?"

Xander stood up sharply. "That's it!" Then he looked about himself, self-consciously, as he realised that the people on the tables nearest to them were staring at his outburst. "Come on," he invited, and left.

"Where are we going?" Rosie asked, once they were outside.

"To get some answers!" Xander stated, grimly, walking quickly in the direction of the tube station. "I think it's time to ask Adon Olam some questions, don't you?"

* * * * *

Back at Xander's house, they were disappointed to find his mum was at home. Rosie and Dan went on up to his room whilst Xander filled his mum in face to face on his results. As soon as he could, he reminded her they were upstairs.

"You don't usually bring friends home, Love. Can I meet them? Who's the girl?" she asked, looking hopefully at him.

"They're just friends. We're going to hang out to celebrate, you know, listen to music and stuff. Can they stay for lunch? I'll introduce them then."

"Ok Love," she looked appeased. "Do you want anything now?"

"No thanks, we're fine. We've just come from the coffee shop." He backed out of the kitchen before taking the stairs two at a time and shutting his door firmly.

"Sorry about that, you know what the folks are like; want to know everything!" He rolled his eyes and smiled at his friends.

"Yeah!" Dan smiled back. "Know what you mean bro'."

Xander turned on the IPod docked on his desk, to provide some background noise.

"Let's see where this gets us," he suggested as he sat next to Dan on his bed. Rosie had swung the desk chair round to face them and he was slightly embarrassed to see her surreptitiously checking out his room. He gave it a quick visual sweep himself, relieved that there were no discarded undies lying on the floor. He took a deep breath, trying to concentrate on the matter in hand. They focused their minds collectively on a return to Olam.

Chapter 49: Olam Again

It was a relief to discover they had all made it through to the realm of Olam. They had not been together here since their training and it did feel different. It was familiar now and held no fear for them. They noticed at once that each other's flames were altered slightly. Rosie's was tinged with green and yellow, as though she were burning copper and sodium within it. Dan's was blue and violet and Xander's flame burned with a mixture of orange and indigo. They were encouraged to see these changes.

"But what about the red?" Rosie pointed out.

As if in response to her question, a voice behind them sang out. "Here I am."

They spun around to see the Spirit of Truth looking more radiant and magnificent than ever.

"Are you here to complete our education?" Xander inquired. "Because we have something we wish to discuss with Adon Olam."

"The Overseer cannot see you now. He is engaged in a matter of grave importance."

"This is important!" Dan spoke with a hint of petulance, but they all felt his frustration.

"Then you may speak it to me." The Spirit nodded graciously, revealing both the masculine and feminine sides of him/herself with equal amounts; like the measured rotation of an oscillating pendulum.

"We think we have uncovered something worrying about Nixon's plans for the Collective. We want your take on it," Xander stated, matter-of-factly.

"Go on," urged the Spirit, gently.

"He appears to have devised some kind of contract for the organisation. Is it possible that this is linked to the beast he serves?"

A look of grave concern was clearly visible on both of the Spirit's beautiful faces. "How could we have missed this? It makes perfect sense!"

"What do you mean?" Rosie challenged.

"The beast you are referring to is Moloch, an ancient god. He reigns over Machon, the realm of destructive ideas, and he has found a way to infiltrate our realms. His partnership with Nixon is stronger than any we have seen between our realm and yours in all of time. It seems Nixon has found a way to perfect the modern day child sacrifice, by requiring that the parents sign an agreement to enable their children to participate in the Collective. We did not see it. We were thinking too literally and expecting him to continue to sate the beast with the occasional blood sacrifice as he has done up until now. Thank you."

"But what do we do now?" asked Dan, shrugging his shoulders helplessly.

"I'm sorry, but there is nothing you can do at this time. I will be in contact with you all soon. I must go. Again, I thank you." The Spirit bowed and was gone.

The children were surprised to find that they had not immediately returned to the natural realm.

"Why are we still here if there's nothing we can do?" Rosie asked, perceptively.

"Because there is something we can do. We just need to figure out what."

* * * * *

Tzadok looked down on the three young people and smiled.

"They are smart, my Lord Overseer. You did well selecting them."

"It was the Brightness that chose them, my friend. Now we wait to see what they have learnt."

Chapter 50: Busted

"What is it?" Nixon demanded, impatiently.

"Forgive the intrusion, Master, but there is something that you need to know." It was Naamah, accompanied by another spirit - not quite as luminous, or as beautiful, or as confident as his favourite guide, but a charming creature to behold all the same.

"Where are you based?" Nixon asked the guide. "Is everything in place?"

"That is what I have come about, Master. I am based at Denman's Academy, here in the city. I left my post, briefly, earlier - there seemed to be no need to be there uninterrupted through the holidays."

Excuses! The surest sign of personal failure. Nixon could not keep the disgust from his face.

"What have you done?" he questioned, pointedly. "At least have the backbone to admit your shortcomings."

The guide squirmed uncomfortably. "Forgive me Master," she bowed low to try to compensate for what was coming. "Somebody has been in my room, Sir."

"Explain yourself! Quickly, before I see to it that you never set foot in this realm again!" He was angry now and had risen from his chair. Nixon also felt a trickle of fear try its best to unsettle him. He was not accustomed to this sensation, but he was no longer willing to take anything for granted. He had planned this, he had foreseen it, he owned it top to bottom; there was no place for fear or failure and definitely no place for complacency. The creature before him cowered visibly, knowing that any hope of a lenient response was vanishing fast.

"There was a hairpin on the cabinet my Lord. Someone has attempted to gain access to the papers."

A blackness overtook Peter Nixon, settling in his tar pool eyes, which looked upon the wretched spirit and betrayed the ugliness of his heart.

"And did they succeed?"

"The lock does not appear to have been breached, my Lord."

Nixon stared at the creature. He had a very finely tuned bull-detector, and all of the alarms had been triggered.

"What aren't you telling me?"

The shoulders of the guide sagged visibly.

"The merest corner of a contract was visible from one of the drawers, Master. It is possible they could have pulled it out a little and seen enough to deduce the content."

"And who do you mean, precisely, when you say 'they'?" challenged the Prime Minister, his voice like a titanium ice pick in the creature's head.

"It was Xander, my Lord, and his friend Rosie."

Nixon sat back in his chair as if he had been shoved by an invisible hand. His countenance closed over, but hatred could still be clearly seen in his eyes.

"Get me the Minister for Education," he said, sharply, into the internal phone. "Now!"

Chapter 51: Escalation

Nixon had forced himself to calm down during the time it took for Angela to get Sebastian Eccleston-Wright on the phone. He could not afford for anyone to even detect the slightest hint of any emotion in his voice, or suspect that he had any personal investment in this plan. This was politics after all!

"Sebastian!" he greeted him warmly. "How are things? Just thought I would check in." Nixon had a counterfeit smile frozen on his face and his fingers drummed the desk, but none of this was communicated down the line to the minister.

"Prime Minister, how lovely to hear from you. Are you referring to the exam results? Marvellous, aren't they. It must be reassuring for you to see the positive results of the Collective reflected in the league tables this year. You couldn't have better publicity for it."

"Indeed. Indeed. Delighted. Which brings me to my point." Nixon had not made the call with a clear strategy in mind, which was a rare thing for him. The bumbling fool on the other end of the line had actually done something useful, for once; he had given Nixon a way in and like the parasite he was, the Prime Minister took no time in pouncing on the opportunity and reeling it in, turning it to his advantage.

"We should not waste any time recruiting. I want the Collective to be fully operational from day one. You know what schools are like in September, it takes them till the end of the month to get anything done. Let's strike while the iron is hot; get some positive press generated and ensure that a letter goes out in advance of the school term to every parent of every secondary school child."

"But," interrupted the minister, with some trepidation. He admired the Prime Minister, everyone did, but he had to admit he was a little intimidated by him. "What about the budget, Sir?"

"Sebastian! You worry too much! We'll find the budget. It's vital that we roll with the gathering momentum on this, or we'll be looking at an ad campaign as well - believe me, that will cost more than a few stamps! All schools already have a contract on the premises for each child, waiting to go out in September. We aren't so much requiring a whole new chunk of money to do this, as just adjusting the schedule. I'm sure there will be some people out there grateful for a bit of overtime to stuff a few envelopes and get away from their own kids for a while, don't you think? I can't see we have a choice. On the back of such positive results we'd be foolish not to act immediately. I will draft a cover letter to go out with the contract and email it to you today, then you can make sure it finds its way, with instructions along the lines of what we have just discussed, to all of the schools. I will arrange for an interview or two, keep the media up to date and get the message out. We shouldn't even waste a day here. What do you say?" Nixon had worked himself up in to a frenzy of enthusiasm, to the point where he actually believed his own hype.

Of course, it was a rhetorical question, and whether the dim-witted politician felt equally inspired was actually completely irrelevant. Fortunately, even with his slightly below average intuitive gifts, Sebastian Eccleston-Wright was clever enough to know when to say, "Yes, Prime Minister." He rubbed his free hand across his face at the prospect of the new deadline and the extra work it would entail - he would delegate a lot of it, naturally, but the wheels of government did not run particularly quickly in August and there would be a lot of disgruntled and resentful people (much like himself)who would not be happy to incur the inconvenience of the new timeframe.

He glanced around him at the swimming pool and sunshine at his Tuscan villa. "I will get on to it immediately."

"Good, good. Well, I'll leave you to it then," concluded Nixon, and he hung up.

"Who was that, Darling?" asked a carefully arranged and immaculately swim suited young woman from her inflatable in the pool. She did not bother to open her eyes behind the Chanel sunglasses, although he could not tell. Their marriage was convenient rather than passionate, but it gave her the lifestyle she had always hungered for and it gave him a beautiful and glamorous bauble to dangle from his arm whenever the opportunity arose. "Not work I hope? We've still got four days of our holiday left."

"You may have, but mine is over," grumbled the Minister for Education, petulantly, downing his large whiskey through the rapidly melting ice cubes. "I'm going to have to fly back early."

"What a shame," came back the perfectly timed reply. She did not even try to disguise the impish smile that played briefly across her lips as she let out a contented sigh and allowed her hand to scull the cool water carelessly.

Chapter 52: Why Are We Here?

"So. Has anyone got any ideas?" Dan asked.

"Well, as we are here," Rosie began slowly, "how about we see if we can find the Brightness?"

A smile spread across Xander's face. "Yes, I think you're right."

"Have you seen the Brightness here, Xander?" Dan asked.

"Well, I'm not sure. I think so. Do you remember me telling you about that stream I went up, to the waterfall? It felt so much like the Brightness. When I drank the water it sharpened my thinking in the same way that being on the labyrinths of the Castle did. It's just what we need. It will help us to focus."

"How do we get there?" Rosie asked. It was a good question, to which none of them knew the answer. Xander may have been here a few times, but he didn't know how to find specific places, he had been taken to them before.

"Well, we're here for some reason, so let's start walking and look for a signpost or something. Perhaps we could try to speak to the Brightness and ask it to help us. If that **is** why we're here, then I'm sure we'll find our way."

The three young adventurers walked along a path which, to Xander's mind, bore no resemblance to the one which had led him to the stream. They walked on in silence, all of them thinking their own thoughts, but none of them thinking it was their responsibility to come up with the solution first - and this marked a real alteration in their perception of this place. They knew by now that this world did not operate in such an Earthly way. Self-discovery was certainly more valuable than any expectation-driven performance.

Xander's head was a mess of questions and thoughts, like a knitting bag that had been thoroughly deranged by a playful kitten.

"Is this the right way?" he challenged himself. "**Is** there a right way? Does it matter which path we choose if we have in mind our destination? Do all paths lead to the Brightness? That was a bit deep," he mused, smiling to himself as a picture of the three of them dressed like a bad seventies movie cast looking for the path to enlightenment flashed through his consciousness. But the question persisted, nudging the image aside and repeating itself as though it was not an accidental or random thought, but a vital lead. "Do all paths lead to the Brightness?" He said it out loud this time. It seemed to be urging him to think about it and to search for it. What was his gift again? Vision. Was this part of that gift of insight, knowing when to pursue a thought and when to let it go?

"What was that, mate?" Dan was closest to him and had overheard his question without really understanding it.

"Just thinking. I was wondering whether we were on the right path, then I found myself asking the question, 'Do all paths lead to the Brightness?'." They had all stopped walking and the other two looked at Xander, encouraging him to continue. "What if, we can find the Brightness because we are looking for it; not because we need to be on a specific path? What d'you reckon?"

"I think you need to go with this thought," Rosie counselled him, "see where it takes you."

Xander closed his eyes. He knew they should not debate this experience. It was tantalisingly close to something true, he could feel it. It was like casting a line and feeling the lure of a fish. He raised his finger to his lips so the others understood; he didn't want them to frighten off the prize. He concentrated all of his energy on this thought and tried to reel it in. His senses sharpened and he felt that he was pinpointing something legendary, on a multi-dimensional level. His friends followed suit, knowing intuitively what they needed to do. Xander pictured the stream he had seen on his first visit to these lands and focused on the emotions and sensations he had encountered there. A magnification of sensory experience occurred and his whole body seemed to pulse with life and light. It was as if his heart reached out with imaginary hands to connect him with the place he yearned to be. It was like an intimate love song going out from him and the intensity of it surprised and delighted him all at once. Lost in the moment, it was actually his auditory capabilities which first registered the change in his surroundings. He became gradually aware of the sound of water, as if it had travelled from his subconscious to his conscious self - like an alarm waking us in the morning from a deep and profound sleep. He opened his eyes just as his friends did and they found themselves beside a crystal stream.

Chapter 53: The View From Up Here

Tzadok knew that time was short. He had been told that the enemy was gathering ahead of the schedule they believed they were working to. The flurry of demonic activity was not something Nixon could conceal from them as they held a unique vantage point which monitored all of the supernatural as well as the natural realms of creation.

"Are they ready now?" he asked Ethan.

"My Lord High Priest," Ethan responded, bowing reverently. "I am pleased with their progress. They have sought out the Brightness independently, and will receive clarity and purpose there. They are learning how to use their skills and operate counter-intuitively to the way they were educated on the Earth. I am optimistic, my Lord."

"Can they access the waterfall? Everything hinges on that. If they do not ascend it, then we have failed."

"I am confident that Tikkun Olam will be within their grasp my Lord. Between them they have the ability and they have shown themselves more than capable of working together for the greater good rather than trying to lead or dominate."

The High Priest bowed his head and allowed himself a deep and steadying breath, relieved that their faith in the young people had proven to be justified.

"And what of the contracts written by Moloch to fulfil his appetite for sacrifice? Where do we stand?"

Adon Olam had been standing silently by while this exchange took place, and it was at this point that he interjected. "They cannot be allowed to go out, my Lord. We **must** be ready, for there is no time left. Once those contracts start coming back in, Moloch's power will increase beyond bounds."

"Would victory still be possible if we reach that stage?" asked Tzadok, warily. He felt the weight of responsibility, heavy upon his shoulders.

"Still possible I believe, my Lord Tzadok, but unlikely. The realms here would be overrun. There is already a siege on our borders with Machon." Ethan's face said it all and they appreciated his honesty.

"There has never been a time on the Earth for such a desperate need for the Breakout. Nor has there been a time when our realms have been so dependent upon man's success. We have one chance here for the Overlaying. We cannot fail."

The three sentinels looked down upon the Earth from their extraordinary position, their hearts full of love but weighed down by the gravity of the situation. They looked through the layers of their eternal kingdoms, to where a storm cloud of gathering gloom was progressing relentlessly, like the shadow of an eclipse, upon its familiar blue and green surface. The day was advancing with unstoppable momentum. The line had been crossed long ago and the inevitability of this moment was decisive. One way or another, the Earth and their own realms would be shaken to the very core and when the sifting had been completed, what would be left standing?

Chapter 54: The Brightness

"Is this it?" Rosie asked, her eyes shining with wonder and excitement. "Is this the place?"

It had been a long time since she had seen anything resembling the Brightness and she realised with a pang of intense longing how much she had missed it.

Xander smiled at her and the two of them felt the deep connection that the Brightness had offered them in the Castle. "Shall we?" he challenged them both, a mischievous twinkle in his eye. He did not wait for a response, just dived right in, luxuriating in the feeling of the water on his skin, enveloping him in its sustaining embrace. Hungrily he scooped up the precious liquid and drank from his cupped hands.

"Look!" Dan was pointing at him from where he stood, waist deep in the crystal radiance of the stream. His face bore an expression somewhere between incredulity and shock. Xander turned to look over his shoulder, unclear as to what it was exactly that Dan was pointing at. He shrugged at his friend, looking puzzled.

"What?" he questioned, smiling and furrowing his brow simultaneously.

"No," Dan laughed, "It's you!"

Xander looked down at himself, his hands spreading out across his chest in a gesture of self-examination. He was initially agitated by what he saw and his instinct was to try to brush the mixture of purplish-blue and orange, almost invisible flames that had engulfed his whole body off himself. He felt like a Christmas pudding, doused in brandy and set alight and his brain shouted, 'DANGER!' Instinctively he dunked himself down in to the water in an attempt to put the fire out, but as he emerged, where the water ran off him, the flames danced and pulsated with even more vigour. His fear dissipated and he looked at his friends; they too were encased in an almost imperceptible shell of coloured flame. He laughed.

"The Brightness must be feeding our fire!" he claimed, and the thought delighted him and charged him with power. It felt right; where they were, what they were doing, and the Brightness appeared to approve.

The urgency of their recent quest seemed irrelevant to them now as they played in the water. It was as if the gift of childhood glee had been momentarily restored after such a long period of anxiety and joylessness. Again, time was not an issue and they had no idea how long they had indulged in this delightful experience. But eventually, and of one mind, they knew it was time to move on.

Just as Xander had been able to run on the surface of the water as well as swim below it, they found themselves able to travel with great speed and dexterity up towards the majestic waterfall at Tikkun Olam. It was even more beautiful than Xander recalled and the waters themselves created colours they had never seen before as they tumbled in to the pool beneath. A rainbow glowed in the spray that rose up, although there did not appear to be a specific light source like the sun in this place. It was as if the water itself illuminated the spray from below as the Brightness infused it with light. It made perfect sense to see it there, and the sheer miraculousness of it was humbling, reminding them again that this was an other-wordly place where they didn't have to play by the rules.

"What do we do now?" Rosie asked after they had all surveyed their spectacular surroundings. She was conscious of having asked questions like this rather a lot today, but there were so many new and exciting experiences and encounters that she felt no need to apologise for it.

"I'm not sure," Xander replied. "I kind of imagined we would be able to get up it somehow; see what's up there. It's called 'The Healing of the Nations' in English, so it has to be the focal point for our whole encounter, wouldn't you say?" He looked at them for affirmation. As one, they turned their heads instinctively to look up to the place, high above them, where the water spilled over the rocks and cascaded down in their direction.

"Did you try to go up it last time you were here?" Dan asked, not wanting to admit that it looked like an impossible task.

"No, I didn't make it any further than this," Xander admitted. He couldn't see a way up either. The sides of the falls were steep and slippery and the water fell vertically, hiding what lay behind it.

"It reminds me of that shampoo advert," Rosie laughed. "You know, the waterfall in the gloriously coloured rainforest." She swam over to where the natural shower hit the basin of the pool, where she stood up and tipped her head back in to the force of the rapidly descending water.

Suddenly she lunged forwards, crying out with surprise as though she had received an electric shock.

"What is it?" Xander asked, seeing the look on her face.

"I don't know," she responded, warily. "You try it." She urged the boys to come and test it for themselves.

Cautiously, they moved to where Rosie had been standing, grimacing and hunching their shoulders in anticipation of what might occur. But neither of them were prepared for what happened next.

Chapter 55: The Vision

Dan broke away first, followed, a split second later by Xander.

"Whoa!" he exclaimed. "That's freaky!"

All three of them had witnessed an open vision as they stood under the waterfall, but none of them had stayed there long enough to properly understand or interpret it. They had felt it though, the darkness, and it was deeply unsettling.

"Should we go back?" Rosie asked, nervously, secretly hoping that the boys didn't want to.

"We have to," Xander responded, sounding more convinced than he looked. "Don't we?"

"Yeah, I think we need to see whatever that was," Dan agreed. "We've been shown it for a reason; we all saw it."

Steeling themselves and holding hands for both moral and physical support, the three of them immersed themselves back under the harmless looking cascade of the waterfall.

The vision which opened up before all three children seemed to play out as if it was being projected on to a giant cinema screen; in 4D! It began on a huge panoramic scale, which seemed to include not just the Earth in it, but all of the spiritual realms as well. They existed together and yet separately all at the same time, like some futuristic, fully interactive yet somehow invisible touch screen, operating on multiple levels. A dark cloud was building and seeking to engulf everything before them. It was menacing and deep, as though it existed not just in the different dimensions they could see before them, but in different eras and parallel time continuums as well. It seemed to be feeding on these timelines like a malevolent raptor, getting fat on the past and the present simultaneously. It took all of their resolve to remain where they were and not break free from the waterfall, thus losing the connection with the vision.

The Earth was all but obliterated by the advancing canopy. It was not just that it cast a shadow - as a storm cloud would - it actually had a physical presence, tangible and thick with potent devilry. Then their perspective shifted so that they were no longer looking down at it from the elevated perspective they held, but they felt the vision alter as they seemed to swoop down through the cloud on wings like eagles, so they were in the thick of it and could see what was actually taking place upon the Earth. They saw families signing documents in thousands of homes up and down the country. Ultimately they focused in on one particular family, sitting around a table. On it was the instantly recognisable contract they had seen in the filing cabinet. It required the parents to sign over permission for their children to belong to the Collective - where upon a list of the benefits of doing so was clearly itemised. It looked like a harmless document offering something which would enhance the experience of every child and ensure they had the best start in life. What was more worrying though, and this was where the document came in to its own, was that at the top right hand corner of the page there was a small square where the child would deposit a drop of their blood to seal the contract. Of course, it was not presented as such, but as a seemingly innocuous way to avoid mixing up identities and building a data base of children's DNA based on the white cells present in their blood. It would also provide a complete viral history, in the interests of safeguarding students' health. Nixon had thought of everything to camouflage his real intentions. Xander did not understand the depth of significance of blood covenants, but he knew enough to ascertain that this was deliberately and directly connected to the beast, and thereby the darkness.

Rosie pulled out of the flow of the vision and the others followed. She had seen enough and it sickened her to her very core.

"How can he get away with this?" she spluttered, angrily.

"He's found a way, Rosie," Dan replied, trying to soothe her - and himself in the process.

"But blood? It's barbaric! People won't fall for it, will they?"

"He's been very clever. He's linked it directly to play on people's weaknesses. He's made it about identity fraud and public health which most people are paranoid about. He'll probably come right out to speak about it in the media any day now and he'll make it sound like the most natural thing in the world. And, to answer your question; yes, people will fall for it, just as they've fallen for everything else he's dished up!"

Xander was right, they knew he was.

"We can't let this happen. The blood ties will make him incredibly powerful. He can't be allowed to get that far."

"School goes back in about ten days, we don't have long," Dan warned. "Was that it do you think, or was there more?"

"We must go back," Rosie said firmly. "Come on," and she pulled them back under the water.

The rest of the vision left them stunned and horrified. They learnt that the letters were being sent out in advance of the beginning of term, so that the children could bring their completed paperwork in on the first day. They saw Nixon receiving thousands of contracts and growing in power and stature until it was impossible to tell where he finished and Moloch began. Threads of light from all across the nation, thousands of them, like fibre optics, rose up and together fused as one in the very centre of the man/monster. There was no time to lose.

"Best case scenario," offered Dan, gravely, "we have ten days to stop him."

Chapter 56: Activation

The three young people were subdued by what they had seen. The vision had stopped by itself - or they had withdrawn from it again, unable to take any more, they could not tell. Either way, they felt it was unnecessary to witness any more. The joy they had felt, frolicking in the water a short time ago, was like a distant and indistinct memory. Like life after a devastating accident. How could you conceive of ever going back to that place of carefree abandonment? They looked at each other but without maintaining eye contact, knowing completely how the others felt. Their shoulders slumped under the weight of discouragement and they waded to the bank of the pool of Tikkun Olam. The waters tried their best to massage some hope back in to them; to wash off the fear they felt; to dilute the bitter taste that the experience had left them with, but without success.

"What can we possibly do now?" Rosie broke the silence with the question the boys had not wished to put voice to.

"There is a reason we have seen this," Xander finally said, standing up on the bank and looking down at his friends. "It's not to discourage us, it hasn't happened yet. It is also my belief that the powers - like the Brightness - which we are engaged with, have shown us what Nixon is up to so we **can** act. Nixon appears to have accelerated his plan because he thinks we saw what he was doing on those contracts. He's always been measured and cautious, historically, careful to get everything in place before he acts. No one suspected him of anything for months and yet he was working away on his plan all this time: finding a way to become Prime Minister; finding a way to get rid of Scarlett; finding a way to ensure he has a binding legacy of support in our nation. But he has altered his plans, and he won't like doing that, so that **must** tell us something," he looked at them expectantly, a twinkle in his eye.

"He's a complete lunatic?" Dan suggested, smiling grimly.

"He's scared?" Rosie contributed.

"Yes! That's yes on both counts by the way, but **yes**!" Xander's voice was raised triumphantly. "He's scared! Scared of failing; scared of us!"

"Of us? Get real!" Dan snorted.

"Yes, of us, his enemy; his opposition; the fly in his ointment! We must not underestimate the power of our position. An investment has been made in us, and others like us I shouldn't wonder, because we are not willing to sit on our backsides and watch him do his worst. What's the saying? 'Evil flourishes when good men do nothing'. Well, like it or not, we're the good men in all of this and the buck stops here. So let's put our heads together and see if we can work out what exactly we are here for."

As he finished speaking, Dan and Rosie got to their feet and looked at him with a mixture of affection and pride.

"I guess Wisdom and Knowledge weren't wasted on you after all, mate," Dan quipped, giving Xander a friendly thump on the back. The orange and indigo aura around him was brighter than it had ever been. "I'm in this, wherever it takes us," he added, realising instinctively that the fear which he had previously thought of as a bad thing was now manifesting itself within him as a healthy resolve and respect for the battle they were in. He was surprised by the sensation that accompanied this epiphany as all at once Dan felt like he was a giant, able to conquer anything that came at him. Simultaneously, his aura of blue and violet took on a new intensity and his eyes flashed with confidence.

"BRING IT ON!"

There was a shift in the atmosphere and they all felt the weighty presence of hope and anticipation.

Chapter 57: Anticipation

The Temple felt almost unfamiliar to Peter Nixon as he walked through the two hundred year old, marble clad atrium in the direction of the Altar Room. He had not frequented it as much over the last few months, as Moloch had made himself at home in a purpose built Throne Room in the Castle. He breathed in the cool air which smelt like a museum and enjoyed the confident ring of his leather brogues on the shiny stone surface as he strode purposefully and with self-assurance past Mitchell, the liveried door keeper who had been there for as long as anyone could remember.

"Evening Sir," bowed the doorman; always the soul of complete, old-school discretion. This place held more secrets than White's - the oldest Gentleman's Club still operating in the city, situated on St. James' Street in London.

"Evening Mitchell," Nixon returned the greeting, smiling at the man. He was feeling excited, buoyant and a little nervous with the expectation of the possibilities so tantalizingly within his grasp. His communications with Eccleston-Wright had allowed him to be more hopeful about the future. By bringing things forward, he had convinced himself that the enemy would be on the back foot, unable to respond quickly enough to the new timeframe. "Is the Altar Room free?"

"As you requested, Prime Minister," deferred Mitchell.

"It is just 'Sir' here, Mitchell, you know that."

"Apologies, Sir. It won't happen again."

"Very good, very good," Nixon responded, barely slowing his pace for the exchange as he walked through to the large mahogany, brass plated doors which Mitchell had swiftly and almost silently succeeded in reaching first, to hold them open for him. He had ceased to notice the Egyptian style carvings around the architrave and the symbols adorning the brass door furniture. The first time he had seen this place he had struggled to conceal his awe, not wanting to look like the power-struck, working class, orphaned young student that to all intents and purposes he was. It was no longer something which impressed him - he lived at Number 10 after all - but it was still a joy to return to this place where his dreams had first taken shape and his mutually beneficent partnership with Moloch had begun. He enjoyed the connection he felt with the men of power who had walked these halls over the last two hundred years; he felt their energy, the ghosts of greatness. But he also felt superior to them, and he basked in the sense of dominance and sovereignty he experienced, to have come from such humble beginnings and owe nothing to anyone but himself, to reach this pinnacle of supremacy.

"See that I'm not disturbed, Mitchell," he added, making no attempt to make eye contact with the man, or even turn around to acknowledge him.

"Very good Sir. Will that be all?" Mitchell's voice could be heard responding as the doors closed behind the Prime Minister and he stood in the engine room of the Temple, the question itself unanswered.

It was a room unlit by natural light except for a stained glass, octagonal dome in the ceiling. The room itself echoed this shape, with one of the sides - the one opposite the large double doors through which Nixon had just entered - dedicated to an altar and throne. Pillars stood at each vertex of the room and the marble theme continued. Either side of each pillar, wall sconces held electric flames where presumably open torches would once have burned to light the room when it was first built. In the centre of each wall, recessed in to the marble, was a fresco depicting various historic battles and painted by the well known military artist of the time, Louis William Desanges. These were added in the late 1840s, after his work had been admired at the Royal Academy and before he moved on to a more lucrative career in portraiture. It was an atmospheric and truly remarkable little know treasure in London and Nixon had spent hours in the early days scrutinising the paintings with much admiration. On the throne, in his usual position, sat Moloch.

Nixon strode in to the centre of the room, where an eight-pointed khatim, or star, was inlaid in to the marble. It was the seal of the prophets and, within the confines of the Temple, precious few were allowed to stand upon it and converse directly with the demon king. At one time Nixon would have knelt on this spot, humbled by the privilege of such a position, but today he did not - a fact which did not go unnoticed by Moloch - but he offered a bow, as one Head of State might acknowledge another without showing any sign of deference or subordination. Anyone else and Moloch would not have tolerated the lack of respect and reverence, but this man was the only one capable of giving him the power he had craved for centuries so he grudgingly overlooked it. All hopes of fathering this man had long since been dismissed and a coolness remained, for they both knew that whether they liked it or not, they needed each other.

"The letters have been sent," Nixon informed him.

"To all students?" Moloch inquired.

"Yes, it has been done. They will bring them in next week at the start of term. We have stipulated that it is to be part of their induction."

"How confident are you of one hundred per cent take up?"

"Very confident, my Lord. People are predictable. There is just the right amount of fear and pressure for them not to realise they are being herded in, but for them to feel compelled to act. Their biggest weakness is their children - a perpetual guilt trip so I hear. I assure you, no one parent will want to feel that they have denied their children either the opportunity of the Collective or its protection. They know that by partnering with me in this, the dominant force in this nation, that is what they will get. I will be launching my public plea shortly."

"It worked for Adolph, you are right. People climbed over each other to sign up their children to Nazi Youth. This is the perfect social climate to launch a movement that gives children a platform and protects them. People will be looking for some stability after such a difficult and unpredictable period. I applaud you, Peter, for your vision and the way you have orchestrated this."

"The blood covenant was a master stroke my Lord, they will tie themselves in unwittingly by sealing the contract in this way. Your power will be immeasurable."

"As will yours, my dear Peter, for you will have captivated an entire generation and assured yourself of their support. Your future is certain. What will you do with them?"

"My Lord?" Nixon questioned, after a pause.

"The children. Do not play coy with me Peter. What do you plan to do with them?"

"The guides will usher them to you. I want to break the weak dependence of the young on their parents. They must learn that they can depend upon no one but themselves - and their guides, of course. I am not interested in them beyond what they can do for me." He smiled to himself. It was not a malicious smile, for his particular brand of evil was not about specifically hurting people as a serial killer might; it was about restructuring society to fit with his warped interpretation of it and put himself in a position of unshakeable power in the process. This was a long game to captivate a generation, one step at a time. He knew he must not get ahead of himself, because that would expose him to the possibility of making mistakes. No, there was plenty of time to consider ways in which he could use his subjects.

Moloch did not want to be a party pooper, but he still had a nagging concern. He had to ask.

"What of that boy?" He spat out the final word in disgust.

"By the time he realises what is going on, it will be too late for him to interfere. He doesn't know that we have changed our timetable of events."

"Are you quite sure about that? The Brightness has been close to that one. He disturbs me."

"I will send out sentinels to investigate if it makes you happier. But I think your worries are unfounded."

"I hope that you're right."

Peter Nixon did not appreciate having doubt sown in to his perfect plan. He gritted his teeth and backed away from the altar.

"Thank you my Lord." Then he turned on his heel and, pushing the doors a little too forcefully as he exited, Peter Nixon left the room and then the building.

Chapter 58: Light

Rosie looked at the two boys, her friends and partners in an extraordinary adventure. She was bursting with pride for them as she saw how they embraced their identities and literally shone. Then a slight twinge of wistfulness came upon her as she regretted the fact that she did not seem to have the same degree of revelation and embodiment of her own teaching experience from the Spirits of Counsel and Understanding as they did.

Xander noticed the change in emotions pass across her countenance, like an errant cloud.

"What is it?" he asked, genuinely concerned for her.

She liked the way he looked out for her, like a big brother, but she felt self-conscious. "Oh, it's nothing," she laughed, "I'm just being silly."

"Tell me," he coaxed. He wanted them to have an equal level of engagement.

"It's just . . . ." she struggled to know how to voice her feelings without sounding petty or immature. "Well, you guys have come so far, you look . . . . I don't know . . . . ready, to me, for what's coming. I just don't feel it myself. I don't want to let you down." Her voice had got smaller as she spoke and she felt herself trying to hide from her disappointment behind an invisible shield.

"Are you serious?" Xander asked, looking incredulously at her. "You really think that about yourself?"

"You should see yourself from where I'm standing," Dan exclaimed having got wind of the conversation. "You look like a kick-ass warrior woman!" He was serious, she realised, and Rosie glanced down at herself. Her clothing glowed with a golden, yellow lustre and she realised she had a kind of cloak on, which shimmered with a vibrant green. She couldn't help but laugh out loud.

"That's who you are, Rosie," Xander looked deep in to her eyes, but for once she didn't break off shyly. Rather she held his gaze and allowed herself to believe it. As the three of them stood there, in full realisation of who they were, the Spirit of Truth descended and covered them with a red glow which had a physical potency like fire. As one, they looked back at Tikkun Olam, the majestic waterfall. It no longer appeared to be insurmountable and impossible. It seemed to be calling them, inviting them to a higher place; to a realm they had never seen before.

As they walked purposefully towards the cascading waters, a shadowy sentinel looked on. He had succeeded in using the turbulent spiritual atmosphere to access the domain which beings like him had never been able to access before. What he saw alarmed him greatly. It was more than he could look at and it sent a chill through him that the Eternal Death himself could not have superseded. What he saw from his vantage point was a vast column of light stretching up in to the heavens and permeating all of the realms of this supernatural world. It was made up of seven vivid colours at its base, but as it rose and the colours mingled, it became a tower of brilliant, white light. He was also aware that other columns of light were simultaneously bursting through the atmosphere at other, more distant locations. He whimpered. Why did he have to be the one to bear and break this calamitous news? For a moment he thought of running, but he knew he would be found. He had come here relishing victory once and for all, but he left in mortal fear.

Chapter 59: Ascent

Previously when they had looked at the waterfall, they had seen it as an unassailable thing. When your head is in control of your decision making and perceptions, then things can be discounted because of how they appear. But now that Xander, Dan and Rosie were operating under the Spirit of Truth, it no longer appeared to be an obstacle for them and they almost flew up it with the same accomplishment as Xander had moved along the path on his first encounter here. At the top, a calmness existed. The atmosphere felt heavier and more fragrant, as though they were in the midst of a tropical rainforest and the water which fed the falls looked thicker and glossier and more iridescent than it did at the bottom. The channel widened ahead of them and seemed to form a large harbour in which stood hundreds of boats. They were tall Barques, a type of multi-masted sailing vessel that was the most popular cargo ship of the mid-nineteenth century.

"Wow! That was not what I expected at all!" Dan breathed.

"You and me both," agreed Xander. "What a resplendent sight!"

"What are they doing here?" Rosie asked.

"They are the Ships of the Nations," a voice behind them said. The three children spun around, startled. Tzadok stood there, dressed in purple and gold, looking every bit as magisterial as the waterfall itself.

"Who are you?" Dan asked, feeling the desire to bow before him.

"I am Tzadok, High Priest of these realms. I have watched your journey closely. You have received a revelation of Truth. It is the only way to challenge the accepted order and see destiny released."

"What are the ships there for?" Rosie asked, feeling bolder than she expected.

"They are waiting to be released. Occasionally, over the course of human history, someone has made it up here like you just have and they deploy a ship for their own nation. This is a unique time, my friends, for more like you are coming and a mighty Breakout is about to take place."

"What is on the ships?" Xander asked, curious and excited about what he had just heard.

"It is the Treasure of the Nations. Each ship carries the destiny of its own land and people. It is your job to release the ship for your country and let it go over the waterfall, so its precious cargo can be distributed over your nation. Tikkun Olam is for the repairing, healing and perfecting of the world and your ship must pass through it if the Breakout is to occur."

They looked back at the lofty vessels in awe as a breeze blew gently through, raising each flag in turn.

"How do we do that?" Rosie inquired, turning back to Tzadok. But he had gone. "Where is he?" she asked, puzzled. "And more to the point, what on earth do we do now?"

Chapter 60: Desperation

Nixon's face and his knuckles, were completely drained of colour.

"What are you talking about?" His voice had a dangerous edge to it and the sentinel cowered involuntarily.

"Something is occurring in Olam, Master. I saw those children and they had tapped in to something, a power. It was like the Brightness, but as I've never seen it before. I could not look upon it Master. It was too dazzling."

"What were they doing, exactly?" Nixon tried to keep the alarm from his voice, choosing instead to pronounce each word with staccato accuracy.

"They were going up that waterfall."

Nixon made a slight adjustment to the position of his head. What waterfall was this? Why hadn't he heard of it before? Why must he persistently find himself disappointed by the ineptitude of those around him who failed to keep him informed about pertinent matters? He fought the mixture of fear and anger that was rising with gathering determination from his gut.

"Indulge me," he almost whispered. His voice may have sounded inviting, but his eyes flashed with a murderous intent. The creature before him shrank back further still from his Master's gaze.

"It is rumoured to be of global significance, my Lord. I do not know its exact purpose and we have not had cause to fear it before as only a handful of people have ever made it up there. But . . . . this was different. And there were more lights in the distance."

"Why has nobody seen fit to mention this before? If this was the object of their quest, I should have been told of it. What is at the top of the waterfall?" Nixon leaned forward, desperate to learn as much as possible. He was a planner and he hated surprises. Being unprepared opened the door to failure and this could not be tolerated. His right hand moved to his mouth, where he stroked his lips - partly from concentration as he waited for the creature's reply, and partly because his brain was already whirring and trying to repair the damage that had potentially been done to his scheme.

"I could not see, it was too bright. I'm sorry my Lord."

"Then we must act now," he resolved, picking up the receiver on his telephone and pressing the button to alert his assistant. "Angela," he snapped. "Call a press conference. Immediately!" He replaced the handset with such force that he heard the plastic crack under the pressure. He glared at it, before grabbing the whole machine and launching it across the room at the cowering demon.

"Incompetents!" he growled. "I'm surrounded by complete incompetents!"

Chapter 61: Darkness

The three young people were awe struck by the size of the magnificent ships, quietly and imposingly docked in the harbour. The sheer number of them was breathtaking.

"There are flags here I've never even seen before!"

"My cousin knows all of the flags for every country," Rosie chipped in, smiling, "and the name of the capital cities. He'd love it here!"

They were looking for the Union flag, or the St George Cross, they weren't exactly sure which. In fact, speaking of not being exactly sure, they had no idea what they would do when they finally did find their ship.

"Is it getting darker?" Dan asked. They had been here for quite a long time already and it occurred to him that there might be such a thing as night time in this realm - although he had never witnessed it on previous visits.

"Yes," Xander replied, looking up. A memory had been triggered - and it wasn't a good one - and with it came a creeping feeling of cold and unease. "Something's wrong."

"What do you mean?" Rosie asked, picking up on the change of mood, her smile and relaxed demeanour instantly being replaced by a tense and worried expression.

"It's déjà vu. Can't you feel it?" Xander responded, recognising the darkness that was rapidly building as the same cloud which had engulfed the Castle. "Not again, surely!" he shouted at the sky, which was indeed clouding over with a menacing intent. "I'm not going through this again!"

"Nixon's up to something," Rosie observed, but Xander wasn't listening. He looked angry and lost and confused all at once, as he waded away from his friends. The action of separation broke their connection and their vision. Each one returned to the Earthly realm and was left to wrestle with their thoughts, their fears and the possible consequences of what they had just witnessed. They sat, stunned, in Xander's room, momentarily paralysed by the extremes of emotions and encounters they were witnessing in such rapid succession. It was draining and baffling to go from such highs to such lows, and to be continually having to read the situation and work out what to do next.

Chapter 62: News Flash

"I'm not going to lose this now!" Peter Nixon stated firmly to his reflection as he sat in the make-up chair at the BBC's London studios, awaiting his press conference. Angela had done a marvellous job of rounding up presenters, journalists and reporters from all forms of media communication. Her connections were legendary and he allowed himself a discreet smile as he thought of the loyalty he instilled in his staff.

The room was empty, as Mandy - the attractive young make-up artist he requested when doing such events - had stepped out to take a personal call on her mobile. She was very good at what she did, but she did like to talk, and at times her South London accent could be a little grating. He valued the couple of minutes of silence to gather his thoughts and prepare exactly what he wanted to say to the nation. He did not write his speeches, as a rule, preferring that they come across as heart-felt and sincere. Nobody wanted to look like George Bush after 9/11! But he most certainly didn't wing it either. Everything he did was calculated very carefully for impact and risk and this was certainly no time to be deviating from his modus operandi. This was going to be one of those defining moments in his life, he could feel it, and he knew just how important it was going to be for the rest of his career and particularly for his dream, that he pitch it absolutely right.

Mandy popped her head back around the door. "Ok there Prime Minister?" she smiled, as only young people with their dream job and no social or personal complications can. He envied her for a split second; envied the carefree, unencumbered nature of her life and personality. Then the shutters came down and the vision took over.

"I will not fail!" he declared silently to himself, like a mantra. The man looking back at him heard though, Nixon could see it in his eyes. He stirred and nodded; he took back control.

"Yes, thank you Mandy. I'm quite well."

"Two minutes to live broadcast if you want to come through and get fitted up for your mic and such."

Giving one last hard stare in to the mirror at the only man who understood what went on in his head, Peter Nixon stood up, extracted the tissue paper that had been carefully tucked in to his collar and strode towards the door, feeling every inch the invincible statesman.

Sitting on a red couch - he had specifically chosen to sit as he felt it would make his announcement look more friendly and relaxed - he watched the countdown to live broadcast. He cleared his throat, adjusted the front of his sports jacket and tugged swiftly at the cuffs which protruded just the perfect distance from the end of his jacket sleeves, then arranged himself casually back on the sofa and called up the trademark Nixon winning smile. The women in the room - and a fair few of the men - looked on with admiration. He was a handsome, commanding figure and he believed, in that moment, that not a single person watching this broadcast would think anything but how lucky this country was to be governed by this man. He was what they had been waiting for; a leader to believe in. And he was right.

The light on the camera directly in his eye line blinked in to life and with an easy charm the Prime Minister spoke.

"Good afternoon," he smiled. "It is such an honour to serve this country and I feel we have reached the optimum time to tell you all about my plans for the new generation."

Chapter 63: Confusion

They were back in Xander's room. He was instantly disappointed as there was precious little they could do from here. He glanced at the clock, it was three o'clock. He thought it would be later after all that had transpired. He remembered he had asked his mum about lunch around three hours ago - had she come up while they were 'gone'? He hoped not. He looked at the others who seemed similarly shell shocked and said, "I just need to check on things, make sure my mum's not suspicious," and left the room.

Xander could hear the television on in the lounge. "Mum?" he called.

"In here Darling," she replied, obviously glued to whatever it was she was watching. Xander pushed the door open and looked in to the room.

"I've just come down to see about . . . . " but he stopped in his tracks when his brain processed the picture on the television screen. "What does he want?" he asked, disgustedly.

"I don't understand why you're so hostile towards him, Xander? He's just about to talk about his manifesto. Do you want to watch it with me?" she asked, turning to smile at him. "Oh, I forgot. What about your friends? Are they still here? You haven't had lunch yet, have you?" She had stood up, suddenly looking concerned. "You were all so quiet up there I'm afraid I forgot about you." She looked apologetic. "Shall I get something now?"

"No, Mum, sit down! Stop fussing!" He spoke more roughly than he had intended and she looked a little hurt. "We're fine, really," he reassured her as she sank back on to the sofa. "Can you pause it a minute? I want to see if my friends are interested in seeing this too." He was already out of the door and climbing the stairs two at a time.

"Yes, of course. It's good to see you taking an interest in politics," she called after him, leaning into the cushions with her head tipped back and to the left.

Xander was vaguely aware that he was interrupting a conversation between Rosie and Dan as he burst in to the room, but there was no time for social niceties.

"Guys, quickly, you have to come downstairs," he urged, breathlessly. "Nixon's up to something and I should think it has everything to do with that cloud!"

"What do you mean?" Rosie inquired, looking a little panicked. "Where is he?"

"Press conference. It's on now, come on!"

Swiftly, the three of them descended the stairs and burst in to the living room.

"My word! You're keen!" Xander's mum laughed, rather surprised by the manner of their entrance. "Have you all decided to do A Level Politics or something?" Nobody laughed. In fact there was rather an awkward silence. "I'm Lana," she said, offering her hand to Rosie, "nice to meet you."

"Rosie, hi, I feel like I know you already," smiled the young girl.

Xander's mum pulled a face. "Really?" She was genuinely surprised, and rather touched that her son talked about her with his friends.

"Yeah, Xander's always talking about his folks," Dan interrupted, to diffuse any awkward questions. "I'm Dan."

"Are you all at school together?" asked Lana.

"We are," Rosie answered, pointing her finger from herself to Xander, "but . . . ."

"Mum, please. We don't have time for the Spanish Inquisition. Can we just see what he's got to say?" He pointed his thumb disdainfully at the television screen as he spoke, as if he had a bad smell under his nose.

"Of course, sorry," Lana responded, sitting down again quickly and looking a little embarrassed. Xander gave her shoulder an affectionate squeeze and smiled at her reassuringly as he reached for the remote to unfreeze the image of Nixon, mid vowel.

Chapter 64: Manifesto

" . . . . 'ew generation," Nixon finished what he had been saying before his speech had been paused. He leant forward, ever so slightly and looked straight down the barrel of the lens.

"Many of you will be familiar with my story by now - in this instant media age it is almost impossible to retain privacy. Of course," his smile was sickly sweet, "I have nothing to hide and it has always - and will always - been my intention to maintain absolute honesty and transparency with you, my electorate.

"Growing up as I did, in an institution like a children's home, has helped me to value the whole dynamic of family life. I may not have had the privilege of being part of a nurturing and loving family, but it does not mean I cannot put measures in place to ensure that children today have the best possible opportunity to become rounded and grounded individuals."

"He's so full of it!" Xander hissed.

"I just don't understand why you are so anti Mr Nixon, Darling. He really is the voice of reason in a volatile time. I think you should listen to what he has to say. It is your generation, after all, that he is concerned with."

"If you only . . . . "

"Shhh," Dan interrupted. He couldn't hear what the Prime Minister was saying. Besides, they couldn't get in to this now; they had to listen and see if he gave anything else away. Reluctantly, Xander conceded. He sat back and turned his attention once again to the screen.

". . . . children of secondary school age will shortly receive a pack in the post, if you haven't already. My purpose for speaking to you today is to help you to understand the significant opportunity currently available to your son or daughter. The Collective was founded by a truly inspiring and altruistic woman, Scarlett Tang, solely for the benefit of young people. She sought to gain nothing from it personally, as it was set up to encourage them to get involved in social and educational issues. I would like to both inform and reassure you that the foundations of this noble concept remain. What we are seeking to do, however - and with no disrespect, this is where Ms Tang failed - is to give **every** child the chance to become part of the Collective. Under her leadership it was rather an exclusive club which a tiny percentage of children were able to access. What I have seen to, is that it is now all inclusive; something your child has as much access to as anyone else. I urge you to fill out the necessary paperwork and sign the contract of inclusion with your children. It will not only help to develop their personal academic abilities, by allowing them to access the subconscious potential of their minds; but it will improve the quality of their social interaction and help to keep them safe from other, more unsavoury influences. I think we all agree that children have too much access to the internet and spend far more time than we would like playing computer games and having virtually experienced relationships. The Collective aims to reinstate the art of communication and interaction, giving them a cause and a focus to take them away from what currently dominates their time and attention.

"I appeal to your maternal and paternal instincts, for although I may not have experienced family life - or indeed have a family of my own yet - I have studied this model and I believe, with all my heart, that it is the answer to problems that have dogged this country for many, many years. Through this initiative, we do not just have the power to provide our children with a safer, more productive and fulfilling environment; we need to remind ourselves that we are responsible for raising the future men and women of this nation - doctors, teachers, CEOs and policy makers. These are exciting times we are in and there is no reason to delay the dawning of a new age.

"Because of the huge numbers of students involved, we have decided that the easiest way to avoid any mix ups is for the child to provide a small pin-prick of blood and to place this on the form, in the box provided, for identification purposes. The additional benefit of this, is that we can scan their blood to issue them with a complete viral history. You would then be notified if there were any medical concerns which may have gone undetected before now, and we would be able to keep track of any potential viral epidemic threats which occasionally ravage schools or places where large populations of people come together. All in all, we are aiming to protect their identity and their health as a by-product of inclusion. The implication that every child is an individual and of value to this nation - worthy of our protection in any and all ways that we can - is embodied in this one, simple act, and I hope you feel able to connect with that message and also see them as such.

"All that remains, is for me to wish you all a restful weekend and I look forward - as I hope you do - to fresh hope in this coming term. This nation has turned a corner and I will not cease in my service of you. Good afternoon."

They sat in silence, knowing that they had just witnessed Peter Nixon at his best. There wouldn't be a parent in the country now who was in any doubt about what they were signing up to; and after such a glowing and persuasive endorsement, there wouldn't be a parent in the country who wouldn't sign it.

Chapter 65: Access Denied

With minimal delay for a quick sandwich at Xander's mum's insistence, the young friends once again retreated to his room.

Dan asked, "Does the power transfer as soon as they sign and seal it with their blood, do you think? Or is it once it gets handed over to the guides in the schools?"

"I don't know. But I think we have to assume the worst. There is not a moment to lose."

"We have to get back to Olam!" Rosie urged.

* * * * *

Half an hour later, after having tried all of the usual methods that they were familiar with, it became apparent to the three of them that there was a problem.

"It must be the cloud!" Xander exclaimed, exasperated. "It's just like the Castle all over again! How can we be beaten by exactly the same strategy a second time? Surely things have moved on from there? Surely we have? It feels like we've moved on, doesn't it?" He looked at them imploringly and they both nodded emphatically, equally disturbed by the turn of events. "It's so damn frustrating! Even after everything we've been through and all we have learnt, we are up against the same old enemy, with the same old tricks and he's **still** beating us!" He was angry and wanted to punch something, but Rosie's presence, particularly, prevented him - it mattered to him what she thought of him, he realised with a start.

"So what do we do now?" Dan was looking at Xander and it was some moments before he realised that he was looking at him for a solution, not just because his gaze had inadvertently rested on him.

"Why are you looking at **me**?" Xander snapped. "I haven't got a clue what's going on!"

"It's ok, Xander," Rosie soothed, "we can work this out together. Don't worry. Neither of us think this is your responsibility." Her eyes were gentle and imploring and Xander stopped pacing around like a caged animal and sat down on the edge of the bed, breathing hard. "Maybe we just need some reinforcements?" She asked it like a question, but Xander knew, instantly, that it was the answer.

"Yes! That's it! Rosie you're a genius!" She blushed under his praise. "We'll go to Scarlett. She'll know what to do."

Chapter 66: Back at the Office

Xander had immediately extracted his phone from his jeans pocket and called Scarlett. She answered on the third ring in a matter of fact tone and Xander didn't quite know if she was busy or just being cautious.

"Hello Xander." No personal greetings or inquiries, which was unusual.

"Hi Scarlett. I'm glad I caught you. Are you free now, by any chance? It's urgent."

He heard her sigh. "Well . . . . I, err . . . . "

"Please, Scarlett. We need your help."

Another pause. "Give me an hour, then come to the office." She hung up.

It was building up to the rush hour as they left Xander's home and took the underground across to Scarlett's office. It wasn't that long since Xander had been here - longer for the others - but so much had changed; he'd changed. Jess had already left for the day and the outer reception area was deserted when they arrived. Scarlett's door stood ajar, however, and she must have heard them approach because she called for them to come in.

Xander was pleasantly surprised to see that she was looking more like her old self - if a little thinner and more circumspect. She stood up to greet them in her red, tailored dress.

"Xander, Rosie, hi and Dan; good to see you all again." She shook their hands in turn, looking genuinely pleased to see them. "Sit down, please," she implored, gesturing with a lavish sweep of the arm to the sofas. When they were all seated, she began. "So, what's the urgency?"

It took the best part of twenty minutes to fill her in on their recent adventures. She looked more and more intrigued as Xander went on - with occasional interjections from his friends. Then her face darkened as they reached the description of the cloud and their inability to access Olam. She was familiar with Nixon's plans, having seen the news, and had been thinking about getting involved again, she told them. Having seen the monstrous Moloch in the flesh, she was determined that they would try to do everything in their power to ensure that he was not allowed to obtain dominance and power over the nation. He and Nixon had to be stopped; of this they were all agreed. Scarlett also concurred with Rosie, that reinforcements were called for. But who? And how? And what would they do with such an assembly anyway?

"So who do we approach?" Rosie asked. "We all know people from the original embodiment of the Collective who we can trust. Shall we start there?"

"I've been thinking," Scarlett suggested, after a pause for communal reflection. "You seem to have had many encounters with the number seven - the realms, the colours, the levels of instruction. What if we gather a committee of seven?"

"I think that's an excellent idea!" Xander exclaimed, feeling a witness within himself to what she was suggesting. "Who springs to mind?"

"I think Lucie should join us," Rosie proposed. She had been a significant figure in the run up to Nixon's exposure in the Castle.

"I agree," Xander said. Dan and Scarlett nodded their assent. "That's five - I'm assuming you're in, Scarlett?"

For what seemed like an age, she stared back at him, expressionless, before suddenly breaking in to a wide grin. "You bet I'm in!" she affirmed, emphatically. "I'd also like to propose my friend Andrea. She's been involved from the inception of the Castle and I trust her implicitly."

"Good, yes; that sounds good. One more?"

"My mate Nathan? He joined us late on in the conference room, I don't know if you remember.

Anyway, he gets it and I trust him," Dan suggested, "I can ask him if you like?"

Xander looked round at the group and felt his hopes rise. They nodded in response as he looked at each in turn. "Yes, do it. That's our seven. Will you contact Lucie, Rosie?" She nodded. "And you two, your friends?" It was agreed. "Let's see if we can all meet here on Saturday then, that gives Lucie a chance to arrange things as she's out of town. I expect tomorrow will be too soon as you and Andrea will probably be working? What do you think?"

"Yes, I can't do tomorrow," Scarlett said. "I agree that Saturday is probably our best bet. Shall we say noon? Here?"

"That's thirty-six hours from now," Xander stated, looking at his watch. "Any problems, contact me and I'll spread the word." He stood up and they all automatically followed suit. Having said their goodbyes, they headed for the lift, reaching for their phones to make the necessary arrangements. The battle plan was in place.

Chapter 67: Nightmares

It was Friday night. Xander had received notification from everyone in the team at various times during the day to say that they were all on target to meet at Scarlett's office the next day. Rosie had also spoken to him privately about a nightmare she had had on Thursday night, involving three hideous creatures who had stood around her, taunting her. A few weeks ago, she would have believed the lies they spoke about her; telling her she was out of her depth and no use to Xander, the weak link in the chain. Although he sensed she didn't need the affirmation, Xander had reassured her of her absolute necessity to the task in hand. She admitted that she had been a little unsettled by the dream on one level - the creatures themselves were menacing and invasive, leaving her feeling violated by their presence - but where she had changed beyond recognition was in the fact that this experience did nothing to shake her resolve or her transformed belief in her own value to the group. He was so proud of her for that. To be honest, Xander was surprised that they hadn't come across more attack of this kind in an attempt to derail or undermine them, but it didn't overly concern him and he went to sleep eagerly anticipating what was to come at tomorrow's meeting.

In his dream, Xander found himself in a room. It was drab and dark and he instinctively felt he wanted to find a way out. He crossed the room and went through a doorway which led through in to a different, but similar looking room. He scanned it, looking for another door but there didn't appear to be one. He did notice something in the corner of the room and inquisitively moved towards it to take a closer look. It was a figure, sitting on the floor with his back against the wall and head bent over his knees. Xander felt uneasy and motioned to leave, but at that instant the figure raised his head and looked straight at him.

"Where are you going?" it asked him.

The face of the man was gray and expressionless, the eyes like dull coals. Xander was first startled, and then horrified, to realise that he recognised the features as those of Peter Nixon - just distorted by the monochrome depiction.

"I'm leaving. I don't have to be here and I have nothing to say to you," Xander responded. He felt surprisingly bold, facing this creature who was unsettlingly more than just the man.

"You don't leave until I say so!" Nixon growled.

At that moment, Xander experienced a strange sensation. It was as if the floor he was standing on was shifting and he felt it in his stomach in the same way that you do when going over a hump-backed bridge at speed. He jumped towards the wall as a spiral of lava appeared, and the centre of the floor fell away to leave a gaping hole.

"I . . . . don't . . . . like . . . . you!" Nixon hissed at him; spittle flying from his contorted mouth and the dark coals for eyes taking on an orange glow.

Xander could feel a force coming from the man which seemed to latch on to his wrists like an indestructible ligature and pull him relentlessly towards the centre of the room and the burning pit. "Your days are numbered and I will no longer tolerate your interference." The man's voice was low and dangerous, with a hypnotic quality which also seemed to be drawing him closer to the danger of the shaft.

"You can't do this!" Xander shouted, panic rising within him. "I'm not going with you and you will not make me! My path is not dictated by you! You are finished!" Considering how mortally afraid he felt, Xander was surprised by how much authority was carried in his voice. He felt no fear by the time he had finished speaking, almost as if his words had purged it from him. Nixon's expression visually altered and he recoiled as though he had been slapped. He stood up with his eyes fixed on Xander as though he was summoning up all of the forces of evil that were at his disposal. The grip seemed to tighten on Xander's wrists and he found he was balancing on the edge of the precipice, feeling the heat of the flames beneath, but what he didn't feel was any alteration in his sense of who he was and his belief in the ultimate victory which he knew to be theirs. He glanced down in to the pit and saw the face of Moloch, the demon king, staring back at him with an expression of intense hatred and anger. His arms reached towards Xander and he seemed to be getting nearer and nearer.

"My offering, Master!" Nixon shrieked. "Take him!"

"NO!" Xander shouted, as the fingers of the outstretched arms brushed his ankles.

He woke up sweating and hearing himself call out in the negative again.

"What the hell . . . .?" he spoke aloud, feeling the need to jump up off his bed and brush the crawling feeling off his skin, like the searching feet of a thousand spiders. He shuddered involuntarily and switched on the light to flood the room with something which could potentially comfort him and slow the pace of his racing heart. It was 4:26am, too early to be up, but too late to contemplate trying to get back to sleep. To be honest, he didn't even want to try; the experience had deeply unsettled him. He went downstairs instead, and turned on the television.

Chapter 68: Seven

Xander felt jaded, to say the least, as he stepped out of the elevator on to the floor of Scarlett's office at 11:48am on Saturday morning. He had already decided not to mention the dream. It had felt so real that he had been unable to even extinguish the light, let alone close his eyes and try to doze again. It had deeply unsettled him and confirmed again the pure evil of the enemy they were up against. Nixon could not be beaten in this realm, that was becoming apparent. He took a deep breath and adjusted his features to appear more positive and optimistic than he actually felt. He knocked.

"Come in," invited Scarlett, breezily. If she too had been awake from disturbing nightmares, then she hid it well. He was relieved to see her in her red battle dress, looking every inch the imposing - in spite of her slight stature - and fearsome female combatant that she was. He laughed, feeling the sudden expression of joyful emotion melting away some of the fear and anxiety of the previous night.

"You look ready to kick some butt!" he exclaimed.

She smiled back with a playful twinkle in her eye. "I selected the pointiest of stilettos for just such a task! Would you care to line them up for me?"

They were both laughing when someone else knocked on the open door and stepped in to the room.

"Ok to come in? What have we missed?" It was Rosie, a smile on her face and Lucie at her side.

"Of course!" Scarlett exclaimed, clapping her hands together like a six year old at Christmas. "Nothing yet, we were just joking around."

The rest of the group quickly followed and after the hugs and handshakes of the reunion had been completed, they sat together on the sofas where so much had already taken place.

They helped themselves to coffee and biscuits, which Scarlett had laid out in advance, then a natural lull in the conversation occurred and led people to glance over at Xander and Scarlett expectantly, waiting for one of them to take the lead. Xander looked at Scarlett too, raising his eyebrows quizzically. She smiled and shrugged in reply, deferring to him and gesturing for him to continue. He cleared his throat, feeling a little nervous. He had not really prepared himself to kick the meeting off, assuming that, as it was Scarlett's office, she would spearhead the gathering.

"Afternoon," he began, glancing down at his watch for confirmation, "just about!" He smiled to break the tension and a ripple of amusement eased its way round the assembly. "Thanks for coming - some of you further than others," he nodded in Lucie's direction, causing her to blush slightly. "I'm sure you all know why we are here. Since our last collective attempt to rectify the damage done by Peter Nixon in the Castle, we have been accessing the spiritual realms and have learnt of a strategy in the heavenlies to not just overthrow this man, but a design for the redemption of the world. We have a very small window of opportunity to access Olam, the realm of the Brightness, and see Nixon and that beast he serves defeated once and for all. We have tried to gain entry as a smaller group, but the gathering darkness of Nixon's evil has come against us and prevented us. In about one week, the contracts which Nixon has issued to every child at secondary school will be returned with a blood covenant tying them in to him and Moloch. At best, we have this small aperture. However, if the power transfer occurs as people engage with the document, then even now his jurisdiction is swelling exponentially. In all honesty, I think this really is our last hope." It sounded melodramatic, he realised as he looked at the pensive faces; like a naff sci-fi movie. But the gravity of their position weighed heavily upon them all.

"There is no time to go through the whole story and the whys and wherefores, you'll just have to trust me on this I'm afraid. Our destination is Tikkun Olam, the waterfall which symbolises the cleansing of the nations. Above it are hundreds of ships; each one representing a kingdom domain. I believe it is up to us to start a chain reaction across the world by releasing our ship of treasures over this land. Once Nixon's guides see this outpouring, they will be very afraid and chaos will ensue - an enemy divided against itself will fall - it is up to us to drive in the wedge of destruction.

"The three of us," Xander pointed at Rosie and Dan, "have received an impartation from seven spirits in Olam. That is why we have called you to be part of this, so we can stand together as seven; the embodiment of the completed work. I would like us all to stand and hold hands, then focus our minds on the waterfall in Olam. Don't worry if you haven't been there, use your Castle techniques of joint visualisation just as you would to support another person's vision on the labyrinth. I will ask the Spirit of Truth to guide us through. Any questions?"

There were none.

"Ok then."

Whether they were specifically chosen for this moment at the beginning of time, or whether they were just seven, random, unremarkable individuals who were willing to lay aside their personal ambitions for the sake of a cause they all believed in was no longer relevant. They stood together in a circle and closed their eyes.

Chapter 69: Olam Revisited

Tzadok stood with Adon Olam, looking down on to the realm upon which the hopes of the nations now rested.

"You are surprisingly calm my Lord," Tzadok declared, his gaze shifting from the master of this realm to the realm itself. One was at peace, the other in apparent turmoil. The river was clearly visible, winding its way like a mercury snake through the land, as were the roads and ancient ways which defined it. But the broiling, ugly cloud that had built up to a bridgehead of apocalyptic proportions, was hard to ignore. It robbed the river of its usual rich and vibrant light and its ability to reflect the glory of the atmosphere here, which would usually resonate with the many colours and vibrations of light.

"Keep watching, my faithful friend," Adon Olam responded, not taking his eyes off the waterfall.

Suddenly, there was a burst of light at its base and an arc of seven distinct and radiant colours surged upwards to the natural harbour which housed the ships of destiny. The overseer exhaled with relief, as though he had been holding his breath for a thousand years of anticipation for this moment.

Tzadok smiled as well, recognising that his master looked unruffled because he had always known this moment would come. "They made it!" he declared.

"They did indeed. Having seven of them was as inspired thought."

Tzadok the priest turned to the Overseer with a wry smile. "And who, exactly, did you inspire with it, Master?"

"Scarlett saw it. She has a special place here and a powerful bond with the Brightness. Many years ago she was chosen and I tied a thread of destiny around her wrist. She saw it and she understood it, but she did not understand its timing. Now the day of Perez, the Breakout, is upon us and she will fulfil her destiny. It is written in the scrolls and the darkness will not overcome what has been promised."

The two lords of the realms of Olam and Ma'on watched in silent satisfaction as the rainbow grew in intensity until it was dazzling against the darkness of the sky.

"The day we have all been waiting for is upon us, my friend," Adon Olam declared. "Come, we must join the Spirit of Truth in the harbour. There is but one chance to execute this and the future of mankind rests upon it."

Chapter 70: An Ecstasy of Access

The spirits of seven very varied, very unique people, left their bodies in a London office block and soared together through the layers of reality and dimensions of supernatural existence as one dynamic and unified light. With each second they felt the power of that unity absorb them in to a cohesive arrow head of strength and intensity. The spirit beings, the angels, the guides and the demons, looked on with either wonder (at the fulfilment of a prophecy) or abject horror (at the destruction of a legacy), as the light source literally scalded its way through the cosmos with a very specific destination. Xander felt as if he had been born for this moment; as if he was suddenly charged with thousands of volts of electricity as in one Planck length of time, every thought, every feeling, every hope and every dream collided in a glorious pinnacle of aligned connection and oneness. He hoped the others felt it to. But how could they not? It was a moment of ecstasy, of perfect revelation, of absolute certainty that all things were finally coming together for good.

As they burst through in to Olam, at the waterfall, every last shred of doubt or fear fell away and he felt himself soar upwards on a wave of expectation and promise that was not just the manifestation of their own hopes, but was fed by the creatures of this realm as well. He looked to his left and right and found he was flanked by Dan and Rosie who, by the looks on their faces, had just had a very similar experience. He could not help himself, as they ascended higher and quicker he let out a whoop of delight and pent up identity which seemed to grow and reverberate with a life of its own, across the skies. He closed his eyes, thrust his arms down by his side, tipped his head back and soared like a superhero in to the atmosphere, high above Olam. It was the purest, deepest, most exhilarating feeling he had ever experienced and when he opened his eyes, he saw his friends were still with him, riding the same wave. Nothing and no one would have failed to notice their arrival.

As one, they descended towards the ships moored in the harbour, their flags fluttering expectantly, like the hankies of families welcoming home their loved ones from the war. Except this was the war; the battle for the Earth, and they were heading straight in to it.

Chapter 71: Fear

Nixon was once again in the Temple, making his final preparations before Moloch.

"Contracts are being signed even as we speak. Blood is being shed for you my Lord, I can feel its power."

"As can I. You have done well," Moloch bowed his grotesque head as a sign of his pleasure. He had grown noticeably in stature and from his hands, blood dripped in a steady ooze on to his lap. He licked his lips, which also showed the residue of blood upon them, relishing the flavour as a gourmet might savour a Michelin starred meal.

Without warning, the Temple appeared to shake. Something which felt like a sonic boom tore through the building. Screams could be heard, echoing through the corridors and up from the bowels of the building - but whether they were human or not, could not be ascertained.

"What was that?" Moloch whined, looking alarmed as the throne he was sat upon was rocked by the blast.

"An earthquake?" Nixon suggested. He hoped that was all it was, but fear forced its fingers down the back of his collar and sent a cold shiver down his spine, leaving him with a deep sense of unease.

"That was not of this Earth!" Moloch spat. "Find out what has happened. Now!"

Peter Nixon did not like to be ordered around; this was his show, he made the decisions. But he felt that something fundamental had shifted and it alarmed him. Reluctantly, he did Moloch's bidding and summoned his chief guide, Naamah.

His fears were well founded, it seemed, for Naamah did not even pretend to be the glorious creature of light which usually presented herself before him. Instead, the cretinous, ugly demon simpered like a whipped dog.

"Speak!" commanded Nixon, angrily, feeling the mask of control slipping rapidly away.

"I'm sorry, Master," cowered the creature. It tried to make itself smaller, consumed by its fear.

"Speak!" reiterated Nixon, desperate now. "Tell me what has happened!"

"They've broken through!" the demon shrieked with despair. "I don't know how they did it, but they've broken through. The cloud did not hold them. There is nothing to be done now, we are finished!"

"What do you mean, finished?" spluttered Nixon, incandescent with rage. "This isn't finished until I say it is! I've waited too long and worked too hard to walk away. Gather the guides, we will eliminate them once and for all! Let's assemble in Olam and kill them where they stand!"

"It's too late, Master. We can't win now. The guides have scattered, run for their lives. It's over!" With that, Naamah scuttled away, whimpering and howling with fear. Nixon felt something rising up in him, an emotion he had long fought to press down and contain. It was something he had vowed never to allow in to his heart again; it was the despair of abandonment. He let out a roar of anger and loss that echoed, not just around the Temple, but through the realms of the heavens as well.

From their position in the harbour, seven adventurers and countless spirit beings - including the Overseer and the Priest of Ma'on - heard the desperate shout.

"In the face of fulfilled destiny and the release of true identity, what more can your enemy do?" Tzadok uttered, wisely. They have seen the Truth that you have seen, and they have run from it. The way is clear for you now to release the Treasure of the Nations."

Chapter 72: A Prophecy Fulfilled

"What you have just experienced," said the Spirit of Truth, gravely, "as you came here, is a revelation of Truth. You needed to encounter that and absorb it in to yourselves in order for you to be in a position to challenge the accepted order of Nixon's regime upon the Earth. What you heard, the screams and cries of despair, was the enemy witnessing your revelation and comprehending that for him, it is finished. What you connected with was what is already inside you; the seed of the sons of destiny. What is coming, what you are here to release, is a worldwide revelation of that Truth. It is a coming together of what has been separate for millennia: the realms of the Earth and of the Heavens. As you release the ship of destiny for your nation, its treasure will be spilled out in a tidal wave of glorious fulfilment over your land and the overlaying of **this** realm; **this** government; **this** authority; **this** atmosphere will be able to finally take place and the two will become one. You are privileged indeed, to bear witness to this moment."

Silently, the seven humans absorbed the words they had heard and connected with the Truth of it; knowing deep inside themselves, in that eternal flame of their being, that things would never be the same again. It didn't matter that some of them had walked the paths of Olam more than others, or had received more revelation about the identities they carried. It didn't matter, because this wasn't about one boy's journey or one woman's dream; this was about the fulfilment of a word spoken at the dawn of time concerning a people who would walk in the fullness of their identities and not under the weight of the deception and control put upon them by others. This was about freedom and they were here to open the gates!

"Do you have any advice for us?" Xander asked their spiritual fathers, feeling the weight of responsibility.

"No. But the fact that you asked that question shows your heart is ready." The Spirit of Truth smiled at Xander fondly and nodded his/her head with the pride of a parent. "You'll know what to do."

The ship was still moored where they had last seen it, near the front of the throng of assembled vessels. As they approached it, they noticed a group, not unlike their own, nearing a boat flying the stars and stripes and another to the ship of an African nation. They were not alone, but they knew they were part of the first wave.

Instinctively, Xander knew he should defer at this point to his mentor. "How do we liberate it, Scarlett?" he asked.

"We must stand behind it. We are not calling it forth, but releasing it, freeing it." They all felt an agreement in their spirits with what she had said. As they moved towards the back of the ship, Xander noticed a thin, vermillion thread tied to her wrist. He had not seen her wear it before.

"Where did you get that?" he asked.

She looked down, surprised by it. She turned her wrist back and forth. "I don't know," she replied, puzzled, "but I think I've always had it."

As they moved closer to their position behind the boat, the thread appeared to become thicker and stronger, looking more and more like an exotic jewel and less like a cord.

Tzadok looked on with delight. "She is in the right place now. She has stepped in to her destiny. Now she will be able to carry the Brightness unchallenged." Nothing brought the spirit beings more pleasure than seeing a person step in to their destiny and, as the seven took up their positions behind the ship of their nation, a shout went up which echoed around the Heavens and will continue to reverberate for eternity.

Chapter 73: The Treasure of the Nations

The seven, glowing ever more brightly, to the point where their seven individual hues had become one white, blinding light, stood behind their ship. A rope moored it to the harbour and Scarlett reached for the hefty loop and released it. They each put their hands to the stern of the ship and instantly felt the connection with it.

"Treasure of our Nation," Scarlett began, "we release you to be distributed across our land. May the identities and truths and promises held back in here until this moment, find their home."

"We declare an end to the old order," Xander found himself adding, "and a beginning to the new Way."

"He has seen it," Adon Olam observed. "I knew he would."

The ship creaked and listed slightly to the left and right before moving off from its mooring with gathering speed. They all looked on in awe as they realised that the enormous vessel was not operating under its own steam, but it was the water itself which was undulating beneath the ship and carrying it forward. Like a countless line of charging horses rearing up out of the harbour, a tsunami of shimmering, living water surged up and conveyed the vessel towards the waterfall. It rose up briefly before disappearing over the falls with a shudder of vibrations which shook the realm they were in and reverberated and echoed on and on, like distant thunder. Shortly afterwards, another ship on another wave followed. Then another and another. It was a powerful and moving moment. Nobody missed the poignancy and privilege of it, and they longed to see its effect upon the Earth.

Adon Olam had come over to join them as they stood on the harbour edge, looking towards the majestic ships rising up and crashing over Tikkun Olam.

"It is done," he declared. "Thank you."

"Will we come back here again?" Rosie asked.

Adon Olam smiled with an expression loaded with all of his years of wisdom and experience. "Wait and see," he responded, with a twinkle in his eye. "Just you wait and see."

Acknowledgements:

These two books have been part of a journey lasting sixteen months, in which I felt the stories of The Brightness and The Breakout gradually revealed themselves to me chapter by chapter. The starting point was a combination of a dream I had a number of years ago relating to having twins, Perez and Zerah (see front quote in The Brightness) and a dream which my daughter had a couple of months before I started writing about a young woman leading children to find a saviour and in the process, their identities. I do not take the credit for imagining this story, it feels like a gift which I am deeply privileged to have been given.

On a personal note, I would like to thank my parents, Karen and David, for supporting and encouraging me throughout this process by reading and proof reading both manuscripts.

I would like to thank my daughter for the original seed of inspiration and for patiently listening to each chapter as it was written - both the first draft and subsequent ones.

Thank you to Rachel and The Big Blake Project for publishing the books for me and to Jane for being a sounding board for ideas. Thank you both for being the first to read the finished manuscripts and feed back to me.

Thank you to Martin Scott for years of inspirational input on turning a town, I have quoted some of your wise words! Also to Ian Clayton for his teaching on the Seven Spirits, a concept explored in this book.

I would like to thank Alex and Steve for graciously allowing me to use the art work they now own the original of to be used for the cover of this book.

Finally, thank you, the reader, for purchasing this book and reading what I hope you will find an inspiring and engaging story about hope and possibility, destiny and love. Bless you.